THE CATHOLIC'S GUIDE TO BEING SINGLE

ALSO BY CATHOLICMATCH INSTITUTE:

Online Dating Guide: A Simple Guide For Catholics

Purposeful Dating

Top Ten Reasons You Should Get Married

The Catholic Playbook: Lenten Reflections For Singles

A Road To Healing: Daily Reflections For Divorced Catholics

THE CATHOLIC'S GUIDE TO BEING SINGLE

By CatholicMatch Institute
Edited by Sue Haggerty

Copyright @ 2015 by CatholicMatch, LLC
All rights reserved.

This book may not be reproduced, stored in a retrieval system, or transmitted, in any form or by any means, electronic, mechanical, photocopying, recording, or otherwise, in whole or in part, without written permission from the publisher, except in the case of brief quotations embodied in critical reviews and certain other noncommercial uses permitted by copyright law. For permission requests, write to the publisher at the address below.

CatholicMatch Institute
PO Box 154
Zelienople, PA 16063
www.CatholicMatchInstitute.com
www.CatholicMatch.com

"We must also remember the great number of single persons who, because of the particular circumstances in which they have to live - often not of their choosing - are especially close to Jesus' heart and therefore deserve the special affection and active solicitude of the Church, especially of pastors."

— ***Catechism of the Catholic Church #1658***

TABLE OF CONTENTS

Introduction xiii

Part 1: Finding Peace In The Single Life 1

Chapter 1: Discovering Your Mission 3

Chapter 2: Following Your Ultimate Goal 7

Chapter 3: Staying Close To Christ 11

Chapter 4: A Call To Holiness 15

Chapter 5: Trusting In God's Plan 19

Chapter 6: Driving Out Self-Pity 23

Chapter 7: Joyfully Embracing Today 25

Part 2: Growing In Virtue 29

Chapter 8: Becoming The Best Version Of Yourself 31

Chapter 9: Building Good Habits 35

Chapter 10: Letting Go Of The Past 41

Chapter 11: Learning How To Love 45

Part 3: Living A Full Life 49

Chapter 12: A Plan For Today 51

Chapter 13: How To Meet New People 57

Chapter 14: Seeking An Adventure 61

Chapter 15: Tackling Loneliness 63

Chapter 16: Understanding Chastity 67

Part 4: Finding Your Spouse **71**

   Chapter 17: Meeting The One 73

   Chapter 18: Taking Risks 77

   Chapter 19: Ten Ways To Prepare For Marriage 81

   Chapter 20: Five Tips for Online Dating 85

   Chapter 21: Tips For A First Date 89

   Chapter 22: Overcoming The Fear Of Settling 93

Part 5: Praying For The Right One **101**

   Chapter 23: Praying For Your Future Spouse 103

   Chapter 24: Praying To Find Love 105

   Chapter 25: Persevering In Prayer 109

Part 6: Looking At The Bigger Picture **113**

   Chapter 26: How To Keep From Worrying About Tomorrow 115

   Chapter 27: Living A Life Of Love 119

   Chapter 28: Why Marriage Won't Solve Your Problems 123

   Chapter 29: Embracing The Life You Are Meant To Lead 127

   Conclusion 131

Acknowledgements **133**

Introduction

Being single can sometimes feel like you are stuck in a Vocation Waiting Area. If you have just entered the waiting area, you're excited and hopeful. Anyone could walk through that door at any moment and call your name. But if you've been in this waiting area for a long time, you might start to worry. Will your name ever be called? You might wonder why God is making you wait. And this uncertainty about the direction of your life can wreak havoc on your personal, and spiritual development, ultimately affecting your relationships.

God's timing is not our timing. Some marry young. Some older. Others date for years before marrying, while some know on the first date, "This is the one." Some never marry while others feel a calling to the religious life.

Your story is your own. You are completely unique from every other person in the world. Yet God has created us all to love. But when you are single, you can feel that you are unable to love fully because you are not married. This is not true. You can love. You do love. Every interaction, every encounter, and every meeting is a chance to love. But sometimes when you feel like you are supposed to be married *right now*, or when you can't even find someone to date, you feel like your life is being wasted. You feel frozen—how can my life begin when I haven't started my vocation?

We understand your questions, your frustrations, and your worry. We want to help you understand that your life *is* right now. The search for a marriage partner can be daunting and lonely. But it doesn't have to be. *The Catholic's Guide to Being Single* will help you navigate this journey through spiritual, and practical advice aimed specifically towards you as a single person. Though your journey may be filled with hardship, and you may be stuck in that waiting area for a long time, you'll find that there is potential for joy. The joy that comes from knowing and trusting that you're fulfilling the life God wants you to lead. Today.

PART ONE

Finding Peace
In The Single Life

Chapter 1

Discovering Your Mission

"We must also remember the great number of single persons who, because of the particular circumstances in which they have to live - often not of their choosing - are especially close to Jesus' heart and therefore deserve the special affection and active solicitude of the Church, especially of pastors. Many remain without a human family often due to conditions of poverty. Some live their situation in the spirit of the Beatitudes, serving God and neighbor in exemplary fashion. The doors of homes, the "domestic churches," and of the great family which is the Church must be open to all of them."

— ***Catechism of the Catholic Church, 1658***

While the single life is not a vocation as the Catholic Church formally defines it, that does not mean you're "vocation-less," or that as a single person, you're any less important in the life of the Church, or any less worthwhile in the eyes of God, or any other conclusions you may draw.

It all comes down to making the distinction between two different but related definitions of the word "vocation." In a sense, there are "Capital V" and "Small V" vocations.

"Capital V" vocation can be used to refer to the Church's formal definition. It is best understood in light of the Vatican II document *Gaudium et Spes*, paragraph 24, which says that "Man, who is the only creature on earth which God willed for itself, cannot fully find himself except through a sincere gift of himself." In other words, we were created to find fulfillment through giving ourselves to another. Giving, not loaning. Permanent self-donation. And that is done, permanently, in two primary ways. The first and most basic way is in giving ourselves to another person in marriage. St. John Paul II, in his Theology of the Body, discusses how the very complementarity of the male and female bodies shows that men and women were created to give themselves to each other. So that makes marriage the "fundamental" way that men and women give themselves to each other.

The second way is through some sort of consecration to God. Priests, religious brothers and sisters, and lay consecrated persons all take a vow to give their lives exclusively to God. They specifically renounce marriage, not because it is bad, but because they have "married" God, consecrated their lives to Him in such a complete way that they are no longer free to give themselves to another human person.

What both have in common is that they are permanent, irrevocable gifts of self to the other (spouse or God). It's difficult in this day and age—when marriages end in divorce and even priests abandon their vows—to conceive of such a complete gift of ourselves. But the Church still teaches that a validly contracted marriage is permanent, and that a priest is a priest forever, regardless of whether he is laicized or even abandons his vows.

In that context, what is single-ness? It is the state of not having given ourselves completely to another. Or not having given ourselves yet. We aren't referring here to those singles who are consecrated. They, in a sense, aren't single anymore. They are "married" to God. But, for the rest of us, our singleness lies precisely in that absence of consecration. I could consecrate myself to God tomorrow. I could get married tomorrow. But, as of today, I have done neither.

The theory is that, in a perfect world, we are all called to give ourselves completely either in marriage or in a religious vocation. But, as we have found, in an imperfect world, things get in the way. We don't find the right person, we don't become the right person, we find the one we thought was the right person and it all goes horribly wrong, etc. God knows that. And He loves us through it.

Hence, the importance of "Small V" vocation. This quite simply refers to what God is calling us to, right now, in the concrete circumstances of our lives as they are. The Church frequently speaks of the "universal vocation to holiness." In other words, we are all called to become holy, to grow closer to God and to allow Him to transform us into what He's calling us to be.

God may call us to many other things. He has called some to speak and write. He has called some to teach, some to take care of loved ones, and some to work in a certain profession or ministry. These aren't "Capital V" vocations—they aren't irrevocable gifts of ourselves to another person. They generally aren't irrevocable at all. A writer can stop writing. A teacher can quit teaching.

"Capital V" vocations are important, of course. If we believe we are called to marriage and we are free to marry, we should remain open to that possibility. If we feel a call to religious life, we should pursue it.

But in our day-to-day lives, it's the "Small V" that matters most. What is God calling me to do today? Where does He want me to serve Him? Where, in His Big Picture, does He want to place me? What is my role? How can I grow closer to Him, and hence more in tune with His plan?

In all of those ways, we "give" ourselves—to God and to others. And if we are faithful in those daily discernments, then we are living lives that are pleasing to Him.

Action Step

What is God calling you to do to live out your "Small V" vocation? Spend a moment in prayer asking God to guide you. After you are finished, write down the ideas that come to mind on a piece of paper. Revisit these ideas over the course of the next 5 days to reflect on them.

Chapter 2

Following Your
Ultimate Goal

"Everything comes from love, all is ordained for the salvation of man, God does nothing without this goal in mind."

— *Saint Catherine of Siena*

For those of us who feel called to the "Capital V" vocation of marriage, but have yet to find the person we will spend the rest of our lives with, waiting can be a painful thing.

It's the type of thing that can lead us down the self-destructive spiral of loneliness and despair. You may ask yourself, "Why am I hurting while others who do not follow His rules seem to get their lives to go the way they want?"

It can make us question our path. "Am I meant to be married or single for my entire life? Where do I belong?" It can even lead to questioning God Himself. "If You're there, why won't You answer my prayers?"

Here's the deal - God does exist.

But the God who automatically provides spouses as a reward for virtuous behavior—He doesn't exist.

Never has. Never will.

It's hard—very hard—to feel called to marriage, to assume that it's your future, and then to find that the "right one" isn't showing up, and to face the possibility that he or she may never show up.

But don't blame it on God.

He loves you. Madly. Passionately. And He wants what is absolutely best for you. More than just wanting you to be "generally happy," He wants you to be really happy. In eternity with Him. Forever. That's His focus. He's our Savior. He came to save us—not from a corrupt government (as many of His followers assumed), or from spinsterhood (as we singles sometimes assume) or from persecution or famine or anything else. He came to save us from the power of evil, and He left us a Church as an instrument of our eternal salvation. And He promised that His Spirit would be with that Church until the end of the world.

As for this life, He never promised us "general happiness," or a peaceful life, or a guaranteed spouse, or anything like that. In fact, He pretty much promised that we'll have a bit of a rough time of it if we follow Him.

You are finding that now. The problem isn't with God, it's with the free will He gave to us. When people use that free will in ways that are contrary to His will, other people get hurt. That's one reason why, in this day and age, so many faithful Catholics are single. Fewer Catholics are taking their faith seriously. And that leaves fewer faithful Catholics for us to marry.

That's not God's "will," at least not in the sense of being what God wants to happen. But He allows it to happen, and people like us get hurt as a result. Being faithful to God has made it more difficult for us to find compatible spouses. That is our cross.

Why don't we have spouses yet when others seem to have received them gift-wrapped from God? We don't know. Why did God spare one family from the Gestapo, while their neighbors perished in the gas chambers? Did God love the one family more? No. He loved both, met each in the midst of the evil they were facing, and fashioned a plan to bring them to eternal salvation with Him.

Challenge yourself to spend some time, in prayer, re-exploring who God really is. He isn't less than the God you're imagining—the one who fulfills your wishes in this life. He is actually so much more than that. He is the God who has loved you from all eternity, and knew from all eternity exactly where you would be in this moment in your life, and has built a plan just for you—a plan to make the most of this time here on earth, and to bring you to Heaven to spend eternity with Him.

That is why you "follow the rules." Not because God promises you a spouse in return. But because you love Him and want to honor Him with your life, regardless of the outcome.

You may still marry. You may not. Either way, God will be with you—loving you, leading you and inviting you into deeper union with Himself.

Marriage is a great good. But it isn't the "holy grail" and it isn't the ultimate goal of this life. Our goal is Heaven.

Keep your eyes focused on that prize.

Action Step

Read the following saint stories. After reading each story, reflect for five minutes on that saint's life. Take a moment to journal about what impressed you most about the life, actions, and/or hardships of that saint. What are the lessons that you can apply in your own life?

Blessed Pier Giorgio Frassati: A fun-loving young adult living during the early 20th century in Turin, Italy, who died at the age of 24 after contracting a disease from a poor man whom he assisted. He had dedicated his single life to serving the poor and sick, advocating for social causes, and maintained a rich devotion to the Eucharist.

St. Guy of Anderlecht: A poor Belgian man in the 10th century who, out of penance for his greed and selfishness, went on a long pilgrimage on foot from northern Europe to Rome and Jerusalem. Despite his economic hardship, he did his best to maintain a grateful disposition all his life.

St. Agatha of Sicily: Martyred in Sicily around the year 250. She was tortured for resisting an imperial magistrate who tried to blackmail her into sex in exchange for not turning her into the authorities for being a Christian. She refused and went nobly to her death.

St. Rita of Cascia: From an early age, she wanted to be a religious, however, her parents betrothed her to a man who was involved in a feud between powerful families in Italy. Rita was married to this man for 18 years before he was murdered. Soon after her twin sons also died and she was called again to the religious life. She asked to relieve Christ's suffering by sharing some small part of his pain. In answer to her prayer, a thorn of His crown penetrated her forehead. She lived the life of a religious for 40 years and died peacefully.

After you are finished with this list, go to CatholicSaints.Info and read more stories of the saints.

Chapter 3

Staying Close To Christ

"Grant me, O Lord my God, a mind to know you, a heart to seek you, wisdom to find you, conduct pleasing to you, faithful perseverance in waiting for you, and a hope of finally embracing you."

— ***Saint Thomas Aquinas***

"I had a lot of fun during the years I was single. I lived in Branford, Conn., close to the beach and had easy travel access to Manhattan and Long Island, Philadelphia historical sites and Vermont skiing. Sunday brunch and a stroll in Central park, going boating on the Connecticut River or having a late night dinner after seeing the Royal Philharmonic Orchestra at Carnegie Hall are some of my favorite memories of being on my own and sharing my time with friends and dates.

But there were always the times when I was alone. Some of these days on my own weren't any big issue, they were more a sort of necessity for regrouping. But often my days spent by myself were overwhelmingly lonely. I didn't want to make dinner for myself, I wanted a table full of noisy, hungry children. I would have preferred to lovingly pick my future husband's socks and underwear off the floor instead of folding my own boring basket of laundry. I was 35 years-old at the time and beginning to feel like I would always be alone.

It was depressing.

However, it was in these quiet times I remember receiving distinct consolations from God — almost to the point of receiving a whisper in my ear — letting me know He was with me and I was never alone.

One of these incidents occurred on a highly frustrating day I experienced. From the time I woke up, my mind was consumed with financial worries, frustrations at work, feeling lonely, and ultimately getting terribly lost on my way to an appointment I was already late for. I entered the parking lot of the office where my appointment was and I broke out in tears. I remember thinking, "I need to talk to someone and just get all this off my chest. Who can I call?"

It was at that exact moment the Holy Spirit inspired me. In my mind I could see an image of the Blessed Sacrament exposed in a beautiful monstrance and heard a voice within me that said, "I am all that you need. You don't need anything else, just Me."

Consolation flooded my heart and I knew what I heard was true. It had been some time since I had spent an hour in adoration of Jesus in the Blessed Sacrament and just had some alone time with Him. Just the thought of being in that peaceful quietness made me feel better. I calmed down and that evening, I spent time in my parish adoration chapel in thanksgiving for His consolations and left my worries at the foot of the cross."

— **Lisa Duffy**

Christ is all you need.

In any circumstance and in every state of life, He is all the sustenance you need. We live in a time where so many people have no idea who Christ is.

Having a good time, being wealthy and powerful seems to be all that matters anymore in society and as Christians, we need to be the leaven in the bread, the light of the world, the salt of the earth. We need to remain sharp and alert. Spending time in adoration will give you all that you need to live in this world full of temptations and distractions.

Action Step

Go to your parish adoration chapel and spend one hour with Christ. Bring Him your worries, hopes, and successes. Ask Him for strength, clarity and courage. If it has been a while since you've been to adoration, distraction is often a struggle. Don't worry about that. When you catch yourself becoming distracted, just bring your thoughts back to the Lord. Some suggestions for a Holy Hour: saying the rosary, reading and reflection on the Psalms, sitting in silence if only for a few minutes, reading stories of the saints, or another spiritual book.

If your parish does not have an adoration chapel, set up a quiet place at home as a prayer corner. Spend the time just as you would in adoration, focusing on union with Christ.

Chapter 4

A Call To Holiness

"All of us can attain to Christian virtue and holiness, no matter in what condition of life we live and no matter what our life work may be."

— ***Saint Francis de Sales***

Focusing on Christ will not only help you grow in holiness, it will help you in your dating life as well.

Our search for the person we're supposed to spend the rest of our life with can be particularly challenging. There are more single people in the world today than any other time in human history. Add the high divorce rate and a host of other issues – it is understandable that frustrations can easily mount. And they typically increase as you get older.

> "Focusing on Christ will not only help you grow in holiness, it will help you in your dating life as well."

As frustrating as it may be to be single and as much hurt and bitterness might have resulted over the years due to bad relationships, heartbreaks, divorce, death or poor choices, the question is: Would you be attracted to you if you could see your own attitude from the eyes of another person? Particularly through the lens of a follower of Christ.

Seeing Yourself from the Outside

Can you see yourself objectively? Some singles are very bitter about their lot in life – and it comes through when they are interacting with other singles. They tend to blame everything and anything on their singleness: Society is a mess. The media is too superficial. Dating websites don't work – and on and on and on.

But is this the kind of person you would be attracted to?

It is not wrong to feel frustrated, sad or even bitter at times. There is real struggle and pain that many single Catholics endure.

But there is a big difference between feeling a certain way and dealing with those feelings versus allowing those feelings to permanently color your personality and, thus, negatively influence the way people perceive you.

The Right Outlook

What do you want people to see when they look at you? As a Catholic single, searching for happiness and finding that special person to spend the rest of your life with is so important. But don't sabotage your chances of finding that happiness by allowing your frustration to overcome and pervade your entire view of life.

Action Step

The next time you act, comment on the internet, or answer someone in a conversation, pause and consider: "If I do this, write this or say this, would I be attracted to me? Would I be inspired and uplifted by my action, comment or attitude?" If the answer is no, then you might be preventing yourself from finding "the one." If you've gotten into the habit of acting, writing, or talking negatively, this can be a hard habit to break. For one day, try and notice all your negative actions. At the end of the day, write them all down. Rather than going through and justifying each action, go through and write down how you could have acted differently. This sometimes requires seeing another person's point of view, using more patience, trying to see the positive even in hardship, or just acceptance of a certain situation. Do this for a week, noting any successes that you've had of responding in a positive way. Also write down the most challenging situations where you struggle. Once you identify those problem areas, be patient with your transformation—pray for perseverance.

Chapter 5

Trusting
In God's Plan

"He who trusts himself is lost. He who trusts in God can do all things."

— **Saint Alphonsus Liguori**

You're improving yourself daily and seeing all the positive changes that you've made. But you're still single. How do you cope? How do you find peace when you sincerely desire marriage and haven't yet found a spouse?

The answer is simple: let go of the idea that there is only one way to be happy in this life.

Many singles only see two paths. Marriage, which of course in their mind would be happy. And eternal un-marriage, which would be bitterly lonely and awful and lead them to long for the blessed relief of sweet death.

Aside from being a vast oversimplification, that kind of attitude leads to a problem. Ultimately you have very little control over whether or not you find that "right" person. But if finding that person is the sole key to escaping a "loveless" life of loneliness and isolation, of course you're going to get increasingly desperate to find him or her. You're going to make yourself crazy. You're going to cling to the hope that God wouldn't do that to you, that He simply must have somebody stored away, and that if you just say the right novena, that person will appear and you can finally be happy.

But it's all based on a big illusion. Married life isn't guaranteed to be happy. And unmarried life isn't guaranteed to be unhappy. In fact, each state of life is going to offer a mix of both.

However, there is a particular cross to the single life. We are made to "be fruitful and multiply," and "it is not good for man to be alone." There is a certain unnatural-ness to the single life.

So how can we be happy in the single state? The answer is to put Christ in the center. With Him, you are never "alone." With Him, life is fruitful, love-giving and life-giving.

Without Christ, the single life looks bleak. But with Christ, there is hope. Pray. Receive Him regularly in the Eucharist. Trust that our Heavenly Father loves you madly, and that He has a plan for your life that takes into account all of the foibles and missteps—a plan for your happiness, and for your salvation. And try to seek His will—not your own—in everything. Everything.

Not that it's easy, or that you'll do it perfectly. But try. And, to the extent that you succeed, your life will be plenty happy and plenty fulfilling.

You will find far more happiness in life if you tweak your thinking slightly. The primary goal of your life should not be to marry. Your primary goal should be to live a life pleasing to God.

So you'll still be dating. You'll still be looking for "The One." But you'll be doing it in a spirit of trust. Not trust that God will provide you a spouse, which He never promised. But rather that He has a plan, and that as long as you remain in Him and strive to follow His will, He will be with you and your life will be fruitful. You may find He has amazing surprises in store for you.

Action Step

Is Christ in the center of your life? Do you trust God has a plan for you? Commit to 20 minutes of prayer every day. This can be all at once in the morning when you wake up. It can be at the end of the day before bed. Or it can be in small increments throughout the day. Here are some ways to spend that time in prayer:

- Have a conversation with God
- Say the Rosary
- Say the Divine Mercy Chaplet
- Read daily devotionals
- Read the Bible
- Say the Creed, reflecting on each line
- Offer God thanksgiving for your blessings

Chapter 6

Driving Out
Self-Pity

"Do not lose courage in considering your own imperfections, but instantly set about remedying them."

— *Saint Francis de Sales*

Trusting in God's plan is not easy. Those frustrations can overcome us and start to affect our personality. We have probably all met miserable single people. They focus on how horrible it is to be single. They talk about being fifth wheels, about not being included in social events, about losing friends when they get married, sighing, "A friend married is a friend buried." They complain that family and holiday events are intolerable because everybody feels sorry that they are unmarried and childless. Sometimes they complain that no one wants to be around them, but maybe you can see why.

For someone who feels called to marriage, remaining single is a cross. Truthfully, though, married life and religious life also have their own crosses. We need to acknowledge the difficult aspects of our state of life, whatever it may be. You don't need to be of the "grit-my-teeth-and-talk-about-how-wonderful-single-life-is" school of thought, but you don't have to wallow in self-pity either.

If you struggle with negativity or feeling sorry for yourself, bring those moments to prayer. When you are challenged at family gatherings, holidays, or time with friends, take a moment to collect yourself. At gatherings of family or friends, don't focus on the children you don't have. Try to concentrate on the blessings you do have: nieces, or nephews, godchildren or neighbors. Focus on your friends, your community, whatever opportunity you have in that moment to be with them and enjoy their company. For particular struggles, ask a spiritual director, or a good friend for advice.

Then during the quiet moments, allow yourself to grieve, really face the reality of your situation and go through the process of accepting it. This is not easy or pleasant work, but with God's help, you can do it. You need to do it to free yourself to enjoy the gifts God has given you, instead of obsessing over the gifts you don't have.

Action Step

Volunteer at a homeless shelter, for your parish food pantry, or a pregnancy center. Helping the poor, vulnerable and disadvantaged helps us to keep perspective and practice self-sacrificial love. After you come home, write down how you felt doing this. Who did you meet while you were doing this? What lessons did you learn from volunteering? How did it make you feel about your own life?

Chapter 7

Joyfully Embracing Today

"I'm still single, traveling around the world, sharing my testimony, trying to work hard in the media, so I can work on projects that entertain but on top of that touch people's hearts and minds, and glorify God in everything I do. ...I'm always open to see if maybe inside of God's plans are for me to marry. ...You try to find holiness and use what the Church gives us to achieve that goal — a life of prayer, a life of meditation, contemplation, loving, giving, serving. Only through that is how you can receive the strength and the grace to love the way God wants us to love Him and others."

— *Eduardo Verastegui,*
star of For Greater Glory, Catholic Digest

Driving out self-pity is essential. Being able to emulate Eduardo Verastegui's attitude by living fully where you are right now as a single person is a gift. Think about it. This moment was given to you by God for a reason, to do what you can for Him in the present. You will be able to do other things for Him when you marry and have a family. So focus on the here and now, now. For as St. Therese says, "The value of our life does not depend on the place we occupy. It depends on the way we occupy that place."

"This moment was given to you by God for a reason, to do what you can for Him in the present. So focus on the here and now."

And as Padre Pio says, "You can't give God deadlines."

No one likes deadlines. They are stressful. They can cause panic as people rush here and there to get everything done. God doesn't like deadlines either. Take comfort in the waiting-for-marriage world that you find yourself a part of—God will send us a spouse at the right time and place.

We must always be "Called to Hope," as Emily Stimpson recently reminded Catholic singles in a National Catholic Register column: "No matter how old we are, if we believe we're called to the vocation of marriage, we can never stop hoping God will send the right someone along. Maybe we can stop expecting, but we can never stop hoping. ...Despair is not our friend. Hope is our friend. Hope is what gets us through a string of bad dates or a stretch of none at all. Hope is what keeps us going after a breakup or when we feel like the last single person standing. Hope is what allows us to trust that God really does know what He's doing."

Yes, He does. In the meantime, joyfully live the single life God has given you.

Action Step

Recognize that for some people being hopeful comes naturally. For others, it is a real challenge. If you find you are having trouble, start small. When a negative thought comes into your head, do not give it space. Instead force yourself to see a positive in the same situation, no matter how small it may be. By doing this continuously, we start to change our thought patterns and outlook on life. At the end of each day, write everything down - this is a great way to track your progress. Look over what you wrote down - can you identify certain areas of your life that you are having trouble with? Can a past hurt be causing these negative thoughts? Can a spiritual advisor, counselor or trusted friend help you work out some of these emotions?

PART TWO

Growing
In Virtue

Chapter 8

Becoming
The Best Version
Of Yourself

"Pray as though everything depended on God. Work as though everything depended on you."

— ***Saint Augustine***

Constantly staying positive about your single life can seem like an impossible task. Single people who wish they were married often feel forgotten and ignored. It's a difficult place to be. Life can be frustrating and lonely, but if you find yourself in this situation you may not realize you are standing on the precipice of a great opportunity...

Before going further, please know that the suffering that comes with the loneliness you feel is real and intense. It's a hardship that many people silently deal with. But there is an upside to your current status.

The upside is the opportunity you have—now, while you are the only one you are responsible for—to work on becoming the best version of yourself you can be. Business owners, artists and musicians, financial investors, and other people who become very successful at what they do often have a simple rule of thumb, and that is doing one thing every day to improve themselves. Let's call it the 1% Rule. If you do one thing every day to be better, however big or small, you improve yourself by 1%, which means, you are always refining yourself. You are getting better every day, just by one small action. This is a great habit to apply to yourself as you wait to meet the one who will become Mr. or Mrs. Right.

This simple concept, the 1% Rule can produce dramatic results in your life and the best thing is, you are the one who is in control of it. You don't have to rely on anyone else.

For example, a writer may do different things to improve his skills on a daily basis; anything from taking a free webinar, generating a list of new ideas, working on learning how to write comedy, etc. Just one thing every day. Not overkill. This will help him to become a better writer. On a personal level, this same man may try to be better by working on forgiveness, working on being patient, being more consistent in his prayer life, etc.

What would a list for you look like? Only you know the areas you need improvement, but here's another thought on this: the improvement you make can be correcting something about yourself you don't like, but it can also be learning new things and taking time to enjoy new experiences.

Here's a list of 13 ideas that could become personal improvements:

- Venture outside your comfort level and contact someone you think is out of your league.
- Attend an early morning mass before work.
- Take a cooking class at your local farmer's market.
- Say a decade of the rosary on your lunch break.
- Work on improving a strained relationship with a relative.

- Take a free teleseminar or webinar.
- Take a walk in the evening instead of watching TV.
- Organize your email inbox.
- Eat healthier food.
- Look up the definition to that word you hear being used but don't know what it means.
- Let someone cut in front of you in traffic.
- Fold your clean clothes right out of the dryer and put them away.
- Clean out your closet.

Action Step

You are the one who knows the best way to improve yourself. Write a list of things that you can work on this week. Use ideas from this list or write your own. The idea is just to form the habit of doing one thing every day to get better. Can you imagine how pleased your future bride or groom will be when you tell them all the things you've done to prepare yourself for a life of love with them? At the end of the week, see how much you've accomplished. For the things that you wrote down, but did not do - what is stopping you? Is there something you can do to make these good habits daily routine? Are you wasting time? Do you put off an important task for tomorrow? Are you reluctant to stretch yourself beyond your regular routine? Answer these questions truthfully and see if you can make small steps to conquering these areas.

Chapter 9

Building
Good Habits

"God does not ask of us anything that He Himself has not first given us. 'We love because He first has loved us' (1 John 4:19). He is not aloof from us. Each one of us has a place in His heart. He knows us by name, He cares for us and He seeks us out whenever we turn away from Him. He is interested in each of us; His love does not allow Him to be indifferent to what happens to us. Usually, when we are healthy and comfortable, we forget about others (something God the Father never does): we are unconcerned with their problems, their sufferings and the injustices they endure... Our heart grows cold. As long as I am relatively healthy and comfortable, I don't think about those less well off."

— *Pope Francis, Lent 2015*

In this message, The Holy Father is talking about caring for the poor specifically, but this mention of indifference often rings true of singles. As a single person, you often have everything you need. If you need something for your house, you buy it. If you want coffee, you make it. If you want to take a trip, you book the ticket. Since you are the only person that you need to take care of, it is easy to forget about others' needs. Singles are independent and often do not need to rely on anyone else. This sense of self-sufficiency is survival mode for a single person, but as Pope Francis points out, does it allow our hearts to grow cold? Does it close ourselves off from others, possibly to our future spouse?

"True friends are humbled to be in the same circle with each other. They see the friendship as a gift and a privilege."

What are the things that might make your heart grow cold? Just by noticing these bad habits can help you start to make a change.

One practical way to practice self-reflection is to ask yourself questions that can help you build good habits to prepare yourself for marriage. The questions are a small reminder to improve every day so that you can be ready to give your heart. By asking ourselves these questions every day, we can start to rid ourselves of any barriers that are holding us back from finding authentic love.

Do I speak kindly?

Observe your interaction with others. Are you sarcastic? Are you cold? Do you need to grow in the ways that you communicate with others? Pay attention to those details and really work on speaking kindly to everyone you meet.

Do I act selfishly?

As a single person, you only have to think about yourself. Most people wouldn't call that being selfish, but just the reality of living in the single state. You have to put gas in the car, you need to buy groceries, you need to pay bills. There is no one else that is in charge of those things except—you.
Married couples with children have constant reminders to act selflessly. For example, a sick child wakes up in the middle of the night and needs care; dinner needs to be made, even after a long day; and don't forget the years of hard work to pay off college expenses! Regardless if they are teenagers or infants, children need so much attention from their parents. As single people, we don't have these little reminders to act selflessly built into our day, so we need to be more aware or make opportunities to serve others.

Do I look for ways to improve myself?

One of the best ways to improve yourself is to deepen and improve your friendships. Developing healthy and strong friendships will help each of us on this journey to discover what God truly has in store for us. And with good friends we don't walk alone.

As true friends journey together, they discover more about each other in a way that is authentic. They challenge each other to strive to become the person God intended them to be. True friends are humbled to be in the same circle with each other. They see the friendship as a gift and a privilege.

As we strive to improve, we don't do it alone when we have good friends. Our true friends help us on this journey. They are there to support and listen, but they are also not afraid to say the hard thing. Real friends will tell you if you need to have a better relationship with your father, if the person you are dating is a jerk, or if it is time to find a new job.

Do I give away my heart and emotions too quickly?

There are some couples who have a fast dating and engagement period while other couples prefer a slower dating process and wait years before they get engaged. The pace of a relationship is not the point, but it is prudent to guard your heart and emotions so you can truly discern what God is calling you to do.

The excitement of new love can have a tendency to make us do crazy things. We want to spend every waking moment with our new found love and learn everything about him or her. We become blinded by this intense connection and only think about when we can see our beloved again. This puppy love phase is just one of the stages our relationships will go through. If our relationship with this person is truly meant to be, our love will mature into a deeper lasting love.

New love is a roller coaster ride. It is fun and exhilarating, but if we stay on the ride too long we might get sick. When we give away our hearts and emotions too quickly, we are in danger of falling into this false love which will only give us more heartache, with scars that are slow to heal.

Guarding your heart doesn't mean hardening your heart either. Pope Francis recently tweeted: "The heart grows hard when it does not love. Lord, give us a heart that knows how to love." Have an open heart to your new relationship, but remember your heart is worth winning. You are worthy of great love.

Do I believe that I am worth loving?

This is an important question to ask. When we doubt that we are truly lovable, we will also doubt that we are worthy of love. This is a huge barrier in finding your spouse. If you don't believe you are worthy of love, you will close your heart and block others from getting close to you. When you don't believe you are lovable this lack of confidence will show through. It is like you wear a sign on your forehead: "heart closed" or "unavailable."

To be ready for someone to love us, we must be convinced that we are truly worthy of that love. If we don't believe that we are worthy of love, how can we convince ourselves?

The first step is to remember that we are made in the image and likeness of God. Our very being reflects the Creator and our dignity is always at 100%. So what does this mean? It means that no matter how we feel, we need to remember and believe that our lives have meaning and importance. No matter how broken, or how flawed we seem, we have a God that loves us so intensely that He is closer to us even than our own breath! If God stopped thinking about us, even for one moment we would cease to be. God didn't create us and then leave us to figure it out on our own; He is active in our lives. He cares about the details and wants you to let Him into your life.

Action Step

In order to successfully change our actions for the better, it is important to truly know ourselves. One way to do this is finding out what is our dominant temperament. Read *The Temperament that God Gave You* by Art and Laraine Bennett. By answering questions at the back of the book, you'll be able to identify your temperament. Each temperament has natural virtues and vices. By identifying areas that naturally you may struggle with, you can get a head start on building good habits. The book also helps you better understand the natural virtues and vices of other people which will offer a glimpse into some of your relationship frustrations.

Chapter **10**

Letting Go
Of The Past

"To love at all is to be vulnerable. Love anything and your heart will be wrung and possibly broken. If you want to make sure of keeping it intact you must give it to no one, not even an animal. Wrap it carefully round with hobbies and little luxuries; avoid all entanglements. Lock it up safe in the casket or coffin of your selfishness. But in that casket, safe, dark, motionless, airless, it will change. It will not be broken; it will become unbreakable, impenetrable, irredeemable. To love is to be vulnerable."

— *C.S. Lewis*

In order to build good habits, we sometimes need to let go of a pain or hurt from our past.

Have you heard the story about the guy with the wooden eye and the girl with the buck teeth?

They grew up in the same town, but didn't know each other because they both kept to themselves, embarrassed by their respective conditions. She kept her mouth closed, never smiling for fear of revealing her buck teeth. He couldn't keep his eyes closed all day, so instead he endured the taunts of "Wood Eye! Wood Eye!" They both longed to find someone who would understand.

They finally met at a party. He saw her sitting alone, and felt drawn to ask her to dance. She saw him approaching, and became hopeful. He didn't speak for a minute. But then, summoning up all of his courage, he managed to whisper "Would you like to dance?"

She smiled a big smile and said "Would I? Would I?"

And he pointed at her and yelled "Buck Teeth! Buck Teeth" She ran away crying and they never saw each other again.

Something similar may be happening, over and over again, with single people and it is holding them back from entering into new relationships.

All of us are old enough to have been hurt somewhere along the road. Some of us more than others. And, like the guy with the wooden eye, we often become defensive. We carry our hurts over into new relationships, and even into casual interactions—online or offline. We assume that the new people we meet are going to do the same things that the old ones did. So we listen for any hint of danger, and then we pounce.

And poor, innocent, buck-toothed girls wind up getting hurt.

The self-protective instinct is understandable. But ask yourself: "Am I projecting old hurts onto new people?"

Take a breath and think before you speak—or type for that matter. Because if you don't, you may be driving away the very person who could help you move past those hurts.

Action Step

Is there someone in your life that has hurt you? Are you harboring resentment from a past failed relationship? Forgiveness is a challenging, but important step in healing. These books will help you through practical advice, spiritual advice and real stories of forgiveness:

- ***The Life God Wants You to Have***
  by Gregory K. Popcak, PhD

- ***Searching for and Maintaining Peace***
  by Fr. Jacques Philippe

- ***Left to Tell***
  by Immaculée Ilibagiza

Chapter 11

Learning
How To Love

"You learn to speak by speaking, to study by studying, to run by running, to work by working, and just so, you learn to love by loving. All those who think to learn in any other way deceive themselves."

— *Saint Francis de Sales*

When reflecting on past relationships, especially ones that may have caused us hurt or pain—we may ask ourselves, "How greatly do I love?"

You may be familiar with the legend about St. Peter fleeing Rome where he met the Risen Lord on the road. When Peter asked, "Quo vadis?" ("Where are you going?"), Christ answered, "I am going to Rome to be crucified again."

In great shame, Peter, the all-too-human apostle, promptly returned to plant the seed of the Gospel in Rome, where he paid the ultimate price with his life.

If marriage is the ultimate "school of love" where, as one of your married friends might say, the "non-relenting demand to be selfless" is ever present, then does being single and living alone foster selfishness? Or worse—mean you are caught in a kind of limbo when it comes to loving well?

This is where "Quo vadis?" comes in.

In the legend of "Quo vadis?" Jesus was not trying to put a guilt trip on Peter. He was not saying that you have to suffer if you want to follow me. But in His reference to the crucifixion – "I go to Rome to be crucified again" – Jesus indicates the depth of the love Peter should have chosen.

Think about it. This legend points to the fact that Jesus loved the people of Rome so much that He was willing to return to teach, to heal and, if necessary, to be rejected and crucified all over again. This is the kind of love that cracks open the human heart. It's the kind of love that Peter immediately understood and by understanding, had to go back to the hard-hearted Romans to preach the Gospel no matter the cost. Peter was a great lover!

You may have a desire to want to follow Christ. You may even want to be a saint. You may want to be a reliable neighbor, faithful friend, a loving son, daughter, brother, sister, cousin, uncle, aunt, granddaughter or grandson. You may long for marriage. All of this can look oh so good on paper but, the question is, "Quo vadis?" Where are you going?

All of these relationships require love. They require that you walk the way of love as Christ taught. As Christ is and calls you to be.

Taking Inventory

It is not enough to want to love. It's not good enough to keep it on paper. Love requires action. Love should be spent generously—no holding back on this one!

Sometimes love is easy—as when your adorable godchild smiles up at your face trying to grab your nose or when Uncle Jerry brags to his friends that you are the best nephew.

Many times love is not easy—like when your grumpy neighbor, who always has a home-fix-it request, grabs you at the most inconvenient time to ask yet another favor or when Aunt Josie, who never gives you the complete grocery list, asks for another run to the supermarket!

As a single person, you are not required to be everybody's valet. It is important to strive for balance in your life. However, the many faces of love often look best on paper, where you don't have to spend a lot of energy, become vulnerable, or give selflessly.

There is comfort in life's routine. There is a type of safety in keeping to yourself. That's OK to a degree, but (and there is always a but), it is important to periodically ask yourself a few questions: How does my personal style of living influence my choices in life? How do personal preferences affect my ability to love? What does my everyday choices say about my discipleship in Christ?

You can love abundantly exactly where you are at every moment of your life.

As Christians, all our life's choices should be colored by loving like Christ. If we play it safe and keep to our routine, the risk is that our hearts will stay the same—or worse, they will dry up and die. The funny thing about the human heart is that it gets healthier, bigger, fleshier, more vibrant with love's color when it is cracked open to love like Christ. And that's the amazing reality of love: Love given to us in Christ is a never ending source of life. It is the road that takes us to eternal life. Eternal life in Him who has loved us so much that He gave His life for us.

And so ask yourself, "Quo vadis?"

Action Step

How can you love more completely today? How can you break out of your routine and stretch yourself to love like Christ? Look at your closest relationships first. Write down 5 names. Next to each name, write something concrete that you can do to show love for these people. It could be anything from sending a card, calling on the phone, bringing over a treat, saying a prayer, running an errand, or just spending time. Then do those things. Once you get through your list of names, start over. Or make a new list. Make sure each week you are practicing self-giving love for the people in your life.

PART THREE

Living
A Full Life

Chapter 12

A Plan For Today

"Do not be afraid. Open wide the doors to Christ."

— **Saint John Paul the Great**

Sometimes, it feels as if life just passes us by without much to show for. This can especially hold true in the realm of dating and relationships while waiting for someone special to enter into our lives. You are God's beloved daughter or son and He has great plans for you. While you wait for Him to show those plans to you, here are things to do now:

1. Pray for Your Future Spouse.

If you don't already, pray for your future relationships—daily! Ask God to prepare you both and to bring you together. Realize that God is the *source* and *author* of all love, joy, and fulfillment. The more relationships revolve around Him, the happier they will be! And, don't just pray to *find* a future spouse, pray that they may be open to God working in his or her life and become the person God made them to be.

2. Keep Hope Alive!

Make a resolution not to give into fear or despair, assuming the worst will happen. "I haven't found anyone yet, therefore, *I never will.*" This sort of attitude will only bring you down. Commit to a more positive attitude of hope and trust.

3. Work on Yourself.

Make a commitment to better yourself in some way. In doing so, you will increase your chances of having better relationships and a happier marriage. Sometimes, a refusal to work on yourself can keep you from finding a relationship—or from keeping one. An extreme fear of intimacy, major control issues, or a lonely neediness can keep you from finding (or keeping) true love. Failure to control your anger, your temper, or your base lustful passions; being too nit-picky, co-dependent, or any host of other problems will keep you from being your best self and can severely injure your relationships. These things need to be dealt with. Have patience with yourself, but you'll be on your way to a more healthy version of you and a better lover.

4. Don't Compromise Because of Fear or Loneliness.

Choose to date only healthy people or none at all! Choose those people who are capable of loving you as you deserve, and don't stay in a relationship you know isn't right. This only keeps you from the person you are supposed to be with. Make a commitment to hold yourself to a high standard, and don't settle. Kierkegaard opens his book *Philosophical Fragments* with the quote, "Better well hanged, than ill-wed." Dating someone out of loneliness or because you're fearful that you will never find someone is always a recipe for disaster. What can you do while you're waiting for that person? See #5.

5. Foster Good Relationships

Sometimes it's lonely and frustrating to wait for a romantic relationship to enter into the picture. While you are waiting though, in addition to Resolution #3, foster good family and friend relationships. After all, dat-

"Make a commitment to hold yourself to a high standard, and don't settle."

ing relationships come and go, but your friends and family are always there for you, even when you get married. So, keep those relationships and don't forget them. Don't be the desperate person who finds someone and immediately makes the other person their whole life forsaking friends and family. Rather, deepen and make lasting friendships which can last throughout your life. Cultivate good hobbies that will keep you busy, keep you around other people, and keep your spirits high. You can take these hobbies into future relationships. Ballroom dancing anyone?

6. Learn From the Past.

If you have found yourself single again in the aftermath of a broken relationship, make it your goal to reflect on your last relationship. What was good? What wasn't good? What lessons can you learn? Especially if the relationship was unhealthy, abusive, or if you were in a relationship you knew wasn't right, take a good deal of time for yourself to consider what mistakes you made and how you can learn from that for the future. If you seem to continually date the same type of people, and it always blows up in your face and goes horribly wrong, there may be a pattern there that you need to consider and pray about. In short, don't repeat the past, learn from it!
Let's make a choice to not only better ourselves in life and to work on those aspects that need our attention, but let us also commit to preparing for future relationships and making them the best they can be.

7. Fall in love with something new.

There's no time like the present to embrace a brand new adventure. Make today the day you learn to love something new. Is there some new challenge you have been interested in that you can take on today? Learn to skydive, take a dance class, join a photography club, or sign up for a white water rafting trip. It doesn't matter what it is. Find some new skill to learn that will challenge and excite you.

Action Step

We have the opportunity to live a full complete life, but that takes work. But a full life is a fulfilling life, especially when it is lived for Christ and others. Take the list above and choose one thing each week and commit to following through. At the end of the month, go through your list. Are you achieving your goals that you set out for at the beginning of the month? Write down everything that you have done. Go over your list. If you're not satisfied, make a new list. Try to commit to things you know you can accomplish. By starting small, you won't feel overwhelmed.

Chapter 13

How To Meet
New People

"Give something, however small, to the one in need. For it is not small to one who has nothing. Neither is it small to God, if we have given what we could."

— *Saint Gregory Nazianzen*

You've been working on yourself and want to live life to the fullest by expanding your horizons. You find yourself on a Friday night. You're fun. You're single. You're up for an adventure. But as you look through your contact list, you discover that many of your friends are married with kids or in a different age bracket and not up for a night out on the town.

Choices for meeting and mingling with other singles doesn't have to be limited. Here are 5 tips to help you not only survive, but thrive as a Catholic single:

1. Resist the Urge to Stay In

Just because everyone on the street has already pulled the blinds at 8 p.m. on a Saturday night doesn't mean that you can't hop in your car and check out a hip new bar or restaurant. Don't let your surroundings diminish your desire to stay active in the singles scene.

2. Join a Supportive Group

Write down your top 3 hobbies and then find a group or a club that fits your interests. Athletic? Join a summer softball league or bowling team. Book worm? Find a local book club or start your own. Encourage others to bring a friend, and you'll be sure to meet new people on a regular basis.

3. Create Your Own Social Scene

The best hang-outs become the best hang-outs because of the crowd. Find a local spot in your neighborhood with a good atmosphere and encourage your single friends to meet there on a regular basis. You may be surrounded by couples and growing families, but chances are there are other singles like you in your area that are looking for some old-fashioned fellowship.

4. Expand Your Search

If you are a CatholicMatch member, you may be tempted to only search for future spouses within a small radius of your current location. By limiting your scope, you may be missing quality individuals who are worth the distance. Numerous CatholicMatch member stories prove that widening your search criteria could be the best choice you make for your love life.

5. Don't Lose Hope

If you feel out of place in your current location, don't lose hope! By engaging in new activities and surrounding yourself with new people, you may find unexpected opportunities. Nothing is permanent unless you let it be, so keep your eyes open for the right path.

No matter what city you call home, don't shield yourself from other singles. Open yourself to the possibility of finding someone down the block or a few towns over. Love can be found anywhere, even while you are doing the activities that you enjoy.

Action Step

Meeting new people can be a challenge! While you may need courage to break out of your comfort zone, act in the hope that each new path, and each new friendship may lead you closer to your destination. Take one of the suggestions from this list and follow through. It may take a little research on your part - finding a local parish that has a singles group, research local community gatherings, or even just following through with a phone call to a friend.

Chapter 14

Seeking
An Adventure

"Spread love everywhere you go...Let no one ever come to you without leaving happier."

— ***Blessed Mother Teresa***

One amazing way to meet new people is through travel. We live in a mobile, connected and fast-paced world. Through social networking tools (and dating websites like CatholicMatch), we can interact with people from other cultures with only a few clicks. But by filing onto a plane and landing in a new city or country, you personally experience life through the lens of a traveler—open-minded and innately curious.

Travel opportunities are endless, and singles, especially, have a unique opportunity to experience new cultures firsthand.

The U.N.'s World Trade Organization estimates that 1 billion people will travel internationally for the first time this year, representing a 4 percent increase from last year. We're becoming more mobile, and it's likely that singles are playing a part in that movement.

There are many challenges to singlehood, but there are also many benefits. Hoping to catch a last minute travel deal? No need to clear the plan with a spouse or feel guilty for shelling out a few hundred bucks. Want to use two weeks of vacation to backpack through Europe? Have your neighbor pick up your mail, and you're good to go.

While many friendships and family relationships take a backseat to marriages, singles can devote time to nurturing these important relationships during an impromptu road trip or relaxing at a tropical location. You truly get to know someone when you take them out of their familiar surroundings, and many times, singles have the flexibility to connect with friends and family in a whole new way while traveling.

Though most of us would likely trade the opportunity to take advantage of a 24-hour fare sale for a loving marriage and growing family, there's nothing wrong with embracing the here and now, while hoping for the future.

So embark on a spontaneous road trip with an old friend. Plan a pilgrimage to your ancestor's home country. Set off on that weekend getaway you've always talked about. Watch 4th of July fireworks in a different time zone. Explore the Rocky Mountains with friends over Labor Day weekend. View singlehood as your passport to new experiences and relish in this unique opportunity to gather as many stamps as you can.

Action Step

Book a trip! It can be a day trip or a week long vacation, just commit to exploring the country and meeting new people! Don't have enough money? Start a savings fund by making small sacrifices. There are plenty of online resources for finding a trip, but if you are intimidated, you can always find a local travel agent. Though they might be more expensive, they will help you find the perfect destination!

Chapter 15

Tackling
Loneliness

"He who possesses God lacks nothing: God alone suffices."

— ***Saint Teresa of Avila***

"*Before getting married, I found it difficult to attend Church on Sundays by myself. After all, Sunday is supposed to be a family day, a day of joy.*

Yet people who are single can often find themselves very lonely. Ever since moving away from my family in Massachusetts and coming to Connecticut, attending Mass every Sunday by myself was tough.

Though I loved Jesus, I still often felt very alone, surrounded on all sides by other couples and families. Sunday is supposed to be a family day, but I felt like the only person who didn't have one.

I knew I would get married someday, but at the time, I wasn't married, wasn't engaged, and wasn't even dating anyone. It was just me, and I felt the weight of that.

To rub salt in my wounds, I then had to go home and eat by myself on the Lord's Day making the loneliness all the more tangible. I often filled the silence while I ate by watching a lighthearted movie."

— *Bryan Mercier*

While you're still in the process of meeting new people, every day can be lonely, not just Sunday. Regardless of the day of the week, here are a few suggestions to break out from the isolation:

1. Grow Closer to God

No one can make you happy except God! No marriage and no person can give you peace or joy that lasts. Every time you experience disappointment or loneliness, it is a reminder that nothing on this earth can satisfy us except God.

As empty as it may feel, it is important, nonetheless, to run even more to Jesus, to cling to Him, and to beg for His peace and fulfillment in your life. Ideally, we should be fulfilled in God whether or not we ever get married. It's helpful to remember that God is love and the source of all love. Thus, coming closer to Him and growing in the spiritual life will only prepare us for a happy marriage and make us better lovers.

2. Hang Out With People

As often as possible, it is helpful to hang out with family, relatives, or friends. If your family is not around, it is important to have positive people you can spend time with. Now, this may entail you doing more of the calling, making plans, and inviting people over for dinner or out to the mall, etc., but doing so is important.

It helps you make that important human connection on a day when loneliness threatens to take over. Even if you hang out with a friend or group of friends in the evening for a short while, this helps because it gives you something to look forward to during the day, the promise of good company to bond with.

3. Get Out

When no one is available, there are other possible options. You can walk around the mall, go to a coffee shop and people watch, take a long walk, etc. Sometimes it's helpful to just be around other people and take your mind off yourself.

4. Employ a Hobby

People who have meaningful hobbies are more likely to put their time to better use rather than just twiddling their thumbs. While it doesn't compare to hanging out with people, finding something you like to do can be a good helpful alternative.

5. Serve Others

Serving others makes us happier and more fulfilled for it is always in giving of ourselves that we receive! So, look for ways you can serve and make a difference (volunteer at a soup kitchen, make someone a meal, help someone in need, etc). As a result, you too will grow and become a better person.

Action Step

Feelings of loneliness can range from mildly sad to severely depressed. When we are trapped in our isolation, we can become paralyzed. But we can only break out of loneliness through action—writing a letter, calling a friend, saying hello to a stranger. Though it may be a long journey, the first step is choosing to do something to decrease your isolation and find companionship. Start out small—give a friendly greeting to the checkout person at your grocery store. Stand in line to say hello to the priest at the end of mass. At the store, ask someone where to find something rather than finding it yourself. These small interactions can make a difference in your life and someone else's.

Chapter 16

Understanding Chastity

"Virtue is nothing without the trial of temptation, for there is no conflict without an enemy, no victory without strife."

— ***Pope St. Leo the Great***

Imagine, if you will, standing at the very edge of a cliff with thousands of feet to fall if you step off, but at the bottom, you will land safely on both feet. How do you feel? If you're like most, you're probably nervous and a little excited. Now, imagine you're right on the precipice—your toes are hanging off the edge and you suddenly hold your head up high, stretch your arms out beside you, and jump! What feelings do you experience? What thoughts go through your mind?

Interestingly enough, this is how others describe what it feels like to make the personal commitment to chastity. Scary! Like taking an extraordinary leap of faith into the unknown.

There are several types of single people who make this decision; those who have never been married, those who are divorced, and those who are widowed. All of them have the same decision to make, but those who are divorced and widowed must pull back tightly the reigns on a passion they've already been able to enjoy. Some people are never successful in getting themselves to take that leap and while others find the courage to do so and act upon the graces God has given them to succeed.

So, why is the decision to remain chaste so hard?

It's difficult, partly because of all the media messages we receive, in particular, the biggest lie of all that if you're not having sex, there's something wrong with you. But the magazines, billboards, television shows, movies and music all attack every sensibility we might have toward living a chaste life. This is sad because there truly is real joy in living a celibate life. This is important to point out for anyone who is struggling with the idea of committing to celibacy until marriage.

Let's say you're standing on the edge of that scary cliff, debating. You don't want to jump because it's scary, but if you don't jump, you'll never reach the solid ground below where you can move forward. You'll always be stuck at the top of the cliff, unable to go anywhere, unable to make any progress. So, you decide taking the risk is better than being stuck and you jump.

You land firmly on your feet and have absolute freedom to move forward. The joy you experience is in the freedom you have gained. But more than that, the joy you experience comes from exercising your free will and choosing to do someone else's will – the will of God, of course. You could indulge in what feels good and what the rest of society says is normal, but instead, you choose to obey God. Not only is that freeing, but it brings an unprecedented clarity to your heart and mind.

Pope Francis did an interview back in 2010 when he was still Cardinal Jorge Bergoglio. The interview was about the "secrets" to living celibacy for priests and seminarians. But his words are important for singles who are trying to live this way, too. Pope Francis admits to the fact that it is difficult, but not impossible. The key is to remind yourself of the choice you have and remember God will not tempt you beyond your ability to resist:

> *Bergoglio: When I was a seminarian, I was dazzled by a girl I met at an uncle's wedding. I was surprised by her beauty, her intellectual brilliance... and, well, I was bowled over for quite a while. I kept thinking and thinking about her. When I returned to the seminary after the wedding, I could not pray for over a week because*

when I tried to do so, the girl appeared in my head. I had to rethink what I was doing. I was still free because I was a seminarian, so I could have gone back home and that was it. I had to think about my choice again. I chose again – or let myself be chosen by – the religious path. It would be abnormal for this kind of thing not to happen (Sobre el Cielo y la Tierra ["On the Heavens and the Earth"], 2012, Sudamericana Publishing Company).

When we resist temptations, especially sexual temptations, it's like reaching a new level of being human. Each time you make the choice to be chaste and resist the temptation, your level of spirituality and maturity is upgraded with powerful virtues and graces that fortify you for the next temptations that will come.

So, have no fear about stepping off the cliff and taking that leap of faith. You will land on your feet and be better, wiser, and happier for doing so.

Action Step

The virtue of chastity is fortified by a strengthening of the will. If this is an area that you struggle with, practice every day to strengthen your will. Wake up the instant your alarm goes off without hitting snooze. Clean your dirty dish right after eating. Give up a favorite thing like chocolate or Monday night football. All these little sacrifices will prove to yourself that you are strong enough to conquer the greater demands God asks of you. It is also concretely strengthening your will against temptations.

If you struggle with pornography, download the Victory App, a new tool in fighting porn addiction.

PART FOUR

Finding
Your Spouse

Chapter 17

Meeting
The One

"What does love look like? It has the hands to help others. It has the feet to hasten to the poor and needy. It has eyes to see misery and want. It has the ears to hear the sighs and sorrows of men. That is what love looks like."

— ***Saint Augustine of Hippo***

There's a story going around about the young woman who made a novena to find a man. Each day she knelt faithfully before the statue of St. Getahunk and prayed the requisite prayers. When the nine days were up and no man appeared, she grabbed the statue of St. Getahunk and hurled it out the window. It struck a man who was passing by. She rushed out and apologized. They introduced themselves, and in due time got married and lived happily ever after.

After hearing a story like this or one similar, too many people believe that the best way to find a mate is to stay home and special order one: simply pick out a novena, click on "free shipping" and wait for delivery.
And don't forget the special features: young and beautiful, rich and dashing. God can do anything, right?

Let's be clear. Prayer is important. Getting married is one of the biggest events of your life, not to mention the riskiest. It has the biggest potential for happiness or suffering. You'd be crazy *not* to pray.

But after you get up and rub the carpet creases from your knees, *do something*. Don't stay home and expect the saints to do your work for you. These people put in their time. They lived in caves, were shut up in towers, or became martyrs. Now is your time.

Fortune favors the bold!

Go to interesting places. Do cool new things. Meet people your age with the same interests. For starters look in your diocesan newspaper and see what's doing:

Golden Halos Knitting Circle? *Pass*. Theology on Tap? *Bingo!*

If you don't have a good local Catholic community, check your local paper too. Go to concerts in the park. Sign up for a class. Join a club. Do these sorts of things and you can't lose because no matter what happens, you will grow as a person.

If you are in a shell, you will need to come out of it. You don't have to be the life of the party—you just have to say hello to people and smile at them. Unfortunately, people often think shy people are snooty. A smile makes you approachable. With any luck, you'll find someone who likes to talk who will do most of the heavy lifting. If not, perhaps you can do a service to someone by putting them at ease. Maybe they're nervous too!

On the other hand, it is possible to act too excited when you see a potential match. Whether you're a man or a woman: don't look overeager. For some reason, being too forward makes people run the other way—a lot like gazelles, only faster.

Instead, meet people in a nonthreatening way, as a friend. You never know who God wants to put in your life.

Action Step

It can be stressful to put yourself out there. It might help you to de-stress if you think about how you met your closest friends. It could be someone you grew up with, someone your brother went to college with, someone you met while serving soup at a parish fundraiser, or someone you wished would just go home so you could put your pajamas on and watch your show. You had no idea that when you met that person he or she would become so special to you. Then CLICK! you *really* discovered the person. Realize that there are just as many ways to meet "the one" you will marry.

Chapter 18

Taking Risks

"Do not look forward in fear to the changes of life; rather, look to them with full hope that as they arise, God, whose very own you are, will lead you safely through all things; and when you cannot stand it, God will carry you in His arms. Do not fear what may happen tomorrow; the same everlasting Father who cared for you today will take care of you then and every day. He will either shield you from suffering, or will give you unfailing strength to bear it. Be at peace and put aside all anxious thoughts and imaginations."

— **Saint Francis de Sales**

"Not too long ago, I balanced precariously on my pink yoga mat in a trendy Minneapolis yoga studio. With one leg crossed around one knee and my arms intertwined, I slowly bent to the left to hold the pose. Some yoga experience may have been required for this class, but it was clear that "some" experience meant more than my casual after-work yoga classes in my company's cafeteria. I stared at the muted yellow wall ahead and with sweat glistening on my forehead, I debated unraveling myself from my awkward *position and walking out the studio door. I didn't, however, and left the class with a feeling of accomplishment. My body may have been in pain, but I pushed myself to try something new and that was something to be proud of.*

I'm not a risk taker. Nine times out of ten I take the safe option, so signing up for this class by myself was a little daunting. As I grow into my later 20s, I'm recognizing my need to push, to challenge and to take risks. I purposely place myself in these types of situations to challenge my preference for the safe, the comfortable and the expected.

During my junior year of college, I followed a recommendation from my Mom to lector at Mass on campus. With a busy schedule and apprehension about the public speaking, I had avoided adding another commitment to my calendar, but I decided to attend the training and act not only on my Mom's advice, but the Holy Spirit's guidance. When I stood at the ambo to lector for the first time, peace washed over me. As I read the words of St. Paul, I made eye contact with several students in the pews. Paul's words had never been as meaningful to me as they were in that moment, and that's when I knew why I was led to take that risk."

— ***Jessica Weinberger***

These risks may appear trivial, but they push us to trust, letting go of the security blanket wrapped tightly around us. As we all know, few rewards can be attained when we're stagnant and unchanging. It's easy to become guarded in romantic relationships, pour ourselves into our jobs and refuse to try something new. Our security blankets can hinder the gentle push of the Holy Spirit leading us to the next adventure.

When we take risks, we display our trust in God. When we open our hearts and surrender all of our hopes and dreams to Him, He pushes us into situations that challenge us but ultimately reward us. The Holy Spirit is our guide in this life, and we can lean on His presence when facing any new experience.

Action Step

You don't have to jump out of an airplane, but each and every day, challenge yourself to open your heart a little more to the Holy Spirit's guidance and God's holy protection. Try taking risks in the direct correlation to a fear that you struggle with. If you are worried about what people think of you, go to the grocery store with two different pairs of shoes on. If you are afraid of speaking to new people, stop someone on the street and ask them for directions. Write down your fears and brainstorm fun and creative ways to conquer them.

Chapter 19

Ten Ways To Prepare For Marriage

"Accustom yourself continually to make many acts of love, for they enkindle and melt the soul."

— ***Saint Teresa of Avila***

Here are 10 ways that you can prepare to meet your future spouse *right now*:

1. Let it go.

Are you holding onto feelings from a past relationship? Let it go and make room in your heart for someone who truly cares about you.

2. Open your heart.

Stepping outside your comfort zone will not only give you the confidence you need, but will help you to be more open to God's surprises.

3. End the dating strike.

Smile, flirt, strike up a conversation. Ladies: Let him know you're available. Men: Ask a woman for her phone number.

4. Don't be selfish.

Marriage calls each spouse to abandon any selfish tendencies. Make choices that benefit others.

5. Keep growing.

Admit when you're wrong, apologize quickly, and work on yourself continuously.

6. Don't settle.

If there is no future with the person that you are dating, and you know you want a future with someone, then, for Pete's sake, move on!

7. Talk it out.

Married couples that communicate effectively say at least five positive comments for every negative comment and work together to draw out each other in loving, effective discussion.

8. Learn to sacrifice.

Remember, marriage is not about you so much as it is about loving and giving to your spouse and kids, even when it's a sacrifice.

9. Sex can wait.

If your relationship is purely based on sex, you become blinded by your emotions, and it is harder to break up with that person, even when you know he or she isn't right for you. Sex speaks a language, the language of forever, the language of life-long love. This is the language of permanent marital love.

10. Be hopeful.

Remember that you are looking for the person you need for a happy marriage, not necessarily the person you think you want. The person you want may not exist or may not be good for you. Be hopeful and pray to understand God's timing for you.

Action Step

Go through the above list. Which on the list applies to you? Write it down. Now add your own ideas to the list. Next to each idea, write a way that you can achieve that goal. Stick the list on your fridge. Keep in eyesight so you can remind yourself what you are working towards.

Chapter 20

Five Tips
For Online Dating

"And then, he got down on his knee right there in the middle of this crowded restaurant, took out the ring and proposed!"

It's wonderful to hear formerly-single people describe their wonderful and unforgettable experiences of getting engaged. The flip side of that coin, however, can be a bit of jealousy. Okay, a lot of jealousy, especially if you've been single for a long time. But we all know that jealousy is pointless when trying to attract the opposite sex. Being a happy person not only attracts others to you, but helps you handle the ups and downs of dating with grace.

In addition to being a happy person, here are some important tips that will maximize your online dating experience:

1. Be Honest About Who You Are and What You Want.

Okay, so you've been emailing back and forth with someone you find attractive and has many of the qualities you desire in a future spouse and it's going very well. You decide to meet for lunch. You are excited and hopeful, but when you arrive you immediately notice that your date's online profile image was very out-dated to say the least. How do you feel now?

There are many ways people can mislead you and no doubt you despise the misrepresentation, so here is a great opportunity to review your own profile to make sure you are truthful in your representation of yourself. Make sure you use your profile to set other people's expectations. Has your appearance changed dramatically since you posted your picture? Post a new picture. Do you agree with only 5 out of 7 questions regarding the faith? Make sure you're honest about that. Your potential dates will appreciate this about you because it lets them know you are trustworthy.

2. Be Interactive.

"I thought things were going well, but all of a sudden, he just stopped responding to my emails. He never gave me any explanation and I have no idea why this happened!" Does this sound familiar?

In order to have a great experience with online dating, interaction is key. Don't suddenly drop the ball in the middle of email conversations or going back and forth about when the right time is to meet. Potential dates really like people who are straightforward with their communication and keep discussions going until it's either time to meet or time to say goodbye.

3. Be Relaxed

Dating is meant to be fun and it's great when you can express your desire to have that in your profile so potential dates have another reason to feel comfortable in approaching you. The website, RandomFacts.com reports that nearly 40% of men do not feel confident meeting a woman for the first time, and since many women still prefer the male be the one to ask for a date, this can pose a bit of a problem. Therefore, make yourself as approachable and as friendly as possible. If you write something like, "I don't like surprises" in your profile description of yourself, how will your date ever dream of surprising you with that totally romantic proposal you will talk about for the rest of your life?

4. Be Flexible.

If an email you sent is not returned with the same enthusiasm in which you wrote yours, or if a date turns out to not be what you had hoped, don't immediately plunge into negativity. Flexibility is important when dealing with people in any manner and especially when dating. If it wasn't what you wanted, expected, or hoped for, just keep going with a smile on your face and your eyes on your goal. Dealing with disappointments using diplomacy instead of blame or negativity is important and increases your ability to handle people gracefully, which is a very attractive quality to have.

5. Be Hopeful.

Keep in mind that God has a great plan for you in mind. Jeremiah 29:11 tells us:

For I know the plans I have for you, says the Lord, plans for welfare and not for evil, to give you a future and a hope.

Especially when you feel overwhelmed or impatient with being single, remind yourself of this scripture passage and place your trust in God's perfect timing. If you feel confident your vocation in life is marriage, then forge ahead with joyful anticipation of what He has waiting for you!

Action Step

Too many take a passive stance with online dating. They sign up and then wait for the action to happen. If this is you, challenge yourself to write one email a week. Respond to messages even if it's from someone that lives outside of your area or your ideal image. Join a forum conversation. You never know what might happen!

Chapter 21

Tips For
A First Date

"One must see God in everyone."

— *Saint Catherine Labouré*

Most everyone who is active in the dating world has funny, embarrassing or horror date stories. Although it's easy to find the humor in them later, when you recount the story, it can be the worst day of your life when you're in the thick of it. From dates that won't stop talking about themselves, ones who keep calling you the wrong name, or ones who ditch you at the table, we can all relate. You probably have some whoppers of your own to report.

There are some things to keep in mind, however, to make first dates a little less awkward. Here's a little list of potentially helpful tips to reduce the stress of your first date and make it as enjoyable as possible:

1. Keep It Simple.

Men: Most women are more impressed by how a man treats her than how original or elaborate the date is. If she feels special, attractive, and important, she *will* enjoy herself so keep the first date simple, and focused on her. Maybe take her to lunch and browse books at Barnes & Noble afterward which is a good way to spark conversation and discuss each others' interests, or maybe a "Movie Night on the Green" if your community offers something like that.

Women: Most men I know like to feel appreciated for what they do, not just for the size of their wallets. If he asks you where you'd like to go, suggest something fun and financially reasonable. For example, many communities offer street fairs or festivals like "A Taste of ... (city you live in)" where simplicity, fun, and wallet-friendly fare are all components.

2. Find Complementary Associations and Experiences.

A lot of people tend to get nervous when the conversation begins to slow down, but this is no time to panic because panicking can easily turn into an opportunity for you to say something stupid or embarrassing. One good way to overcome the pressure to have something to say is by listening closely to the things your date tells you and see if you have any complementary associations or experiences that you can talk about when the lulls in conversation show up. Instead of bringing it up while he or she is doing the talking, the lulls can be a time you can easily turn the conversation to yourself.

3. Have A Sense Of Humor.

Hey, stuff happens on first dates. Embarrassing stuff. Little particles of food come flying out of your mouth when you're talking. Mud splashes on your pants. You intend to say one thing but you get tongue-tied and something different comes out. It happens! Like one guy who reported on meeting his date's father for the first time: He intended to say, *It's a pleasure to meet you,* but what actually came out was, *I am pleasure.* It doesn't get more awkward than that! Be the kind of person who can laugh at yourself without your whole day being ruined. Have a sense of humor about it all so when you look back, it is a pleasant memory, not an awful one.

4. Have A Plan B.

Imagine you go out to dinner, but your date forgets to make a reservation. Or you head to a restaurant and it's closed for remodeling. Or you plan to go a steak house, but your date tells you on the way that she's a vegetarian. These events can put a real damper on an evening. If it takes you a long time to make a decision, than being put on the spot can be incredibly stressful. Men, if you find yourself in a situation where Plan A just won't work, have a back-up plan or two. Ladies, if Plan A goes awry, be flexible, be gracious, and be adventurous.

5. Be Yourself.

That probably sounds like a platitude but you'd be surprised by how far some people will go to make an initial good impression on their date—to the point of being fraudulent. Remember that you've already been endowed by God with excellent gifts and talents so there's no need to rely on anything else but the wonderful person you are. If you are with a good person, he or she will appreciate you for who you are.

Action Step

Remember that dating is supposed to be fun! Don't let your nerves and awkwardness takeover, just keep it simple, plan a little, have a sense of humor and most likely you'll have a great time!

Chapter 22

Overcoming The Fear of Settling

*""I ain't settling for just getting by
I've had enough 'so so' for the rest of my life
Tired of shooting too low, so raise the bar high
Just enough ain't enough this time
I ain't settling for anything less than everything"*

— **Sugarland**

Country music fans will recognize the lyrics to the chart-topping Sugarland song. Whether Sugarland is currently playing on your iPod or you've never heard of the band, the words of their "Settling" song are a perfect introduction to the topic of settling. When it comes to dating, Catholic singles fall into one of three categories on the "pickiness meter" of what they are looking for in a spouse. These three groups of people are:

1. "Picky"

Definition: You have carefully thought through your standards and requirements for what you are looking for in a spouse. You know yourself well, and take into account a person's temperament, personality, characteristics, interests, faith, and worldview, before beginning a serious relationship or deciding to marry that person.

You look for someone who shares a similar desire for marriage and family life—someone who will be your best friend and your partner on the journey to Heaven. You decline the attentions of those whom you are sure would not make a suitable or compatible marriage partner.

Occasionally, friends or family members tease you about being "too picky" when it comes to dating, but you know deep down inside that even though it's difficult to be patient and wait for the right person, in the long run you are being wise in your relationship decisions and will one day be rewarded with a successful and happy marriage.

2. "Too Picky"

Definition: You keep a long and detailed list of exactly what you want in a mate, down to the age, weight, eye color, and favorite sports team. Your friends and relatives frequently warn you that you'll never get married because your standards are so unrealistically high. They tell you that John the Baptist or the Blessed Virgin Mary would not pass your checklist of requirements in a spouse. You find nearly every new person you meet "not good enough" to date. Whether you realize it or not, you are looking for a "perfect" spouse, not just "perfect for you."

3. "Not Picky Enough"

Definition: This category can be summed up in one word: *settling*.

While you know yourself well and know what your "ideal" is in a spouse, you have such a hard time finding single people who meet your standards, even on important matters such as a shared faith, ideas about family life, and common interests. But you don't want to remain single for the rest of your life, so you decide to settle for less than what you had always thought was good enough for you.

You admit to "settling" in your relationships and may even be disappointed in yourself for lowering your standards, but you don't know what else to do.

Should We Compromise on the Important Stuff?

Once there was a young woman that called into a radio talk show that was discussing dating and relationship topics. The young woman said she had been receiving a lot of advice from her friends to "expand her horizons" and start dating men who did not share her Catholic faith. With confusion and a touch of desperation in her voice, she asked the show's guest expert, *"The Catholic faith is really important to me, and I've always wanted to find a guy who shared my Faith. Am I being too picky if I have a personal rule that I'll only date Catholic guys?"*

The show's "relationships expert" responded by telling the woman that perhaps she was too picky, and maybe she should start widening and deepening the pool she was fishing in for a spouse. *"Otherwise, you might end up single for the rest of your life, and it sounds like you really don't want that to happen,"* he concluded.

It is certainly not easy to be a Catholic "single and searching" person in the secular culture we live in. Finding people our own age, who share our Faith and also share similar goals, interests and dreams seems nearly impossible sometimes. While the temptation to start re-evaluating or even lowering your standards may be great, know that you are not alone in your struggles or your anxiety. Take courage that God is with you and He truly wants your dreams to come true and your deepest desires to be fulfilled.

Anxiety about being too picky in your search for a spouse is one of the reasons CatholicMatch.com exists. This is a place where single Catholics from all over the world can come together and find community, support, encouragement, good (sometimes even challenging) advice, and, if it is God's will, the spouse of your dreams. When you become anxious or despondent about relationships, visit the forums or community rooms on CatholicMatch and be encouraged that there are literally thousands of single Catholics in the world today, searching just like you, but also willing to be patient and wait for God's best in their lives.

"Take courage that God is with you and He truly wants your dreams to come true and your deepest desires to be fulfilled."

If you feel that you might fall into the "not picky enough" category when it comes to dating, perhaps now is a good time to "raise the bar high" as Sugarland sings, and re-examine your priorities and perspectives on dating and choosing a spouse. Following are some helpful tips for elevating your standards:

If You've Compromised with Yourself, Renegotiate

Do not compromise on the important stuff. Sure, many of us probably have items on our "spouse wish list" that are unrealistic, and in that case we truly *do* need to give the Holy Spirit a little more room to work in our lives. However, there are certain aspects or traits in a person that you know beyond a doubt are important to you. You know that "giving in" on these areas is lowering your standards, or settling for less than what you are really looking for.

These "important standards" are not just faith compatibility in a relationship. Just because a person is Catholic, or shares your faith, does not mean that the two of you would make a great marriage. There might be several other areas of life that are truly "must haves" or "can't stands" for you, and it's completely okay to make those things part of your standards for a relationship.

If you feel that you have begun compromising on important issues in your dating relationships, revisit your standards and make a renewed commitment to avoid settling.

Pray for Discernment, and for Patience

If you ask Him for it, your Heavenly Father will give you a discerning heart to know what His will is for your life. Ask specifically for wisdom in creating your list of standards when choosing a spouse, and He will supply your needs.

Also, ask God to give you the virtue of patience, which is intimately connected to wisdom and endurance in difficult times. The dictionary definition of patience is: "1) bearing pains or trials calmly or without complaint; 2) manifesting forbearance under provocation or strain; 3) not hasty or impetuous; 4) steadfast despite opposition, difficulty, or adversity" *(Merriam-Webster)*.

All of the above definitions remind us that being patient is a difficult struggle, and oftentimes it hurts. However, the Bible is very clear that there is great reward and blessing in store for those who patiently endure trials. The Book of Sirach states: "A patient man will endure until the right moment, and then joy will burst forth for him" (1:23). King David reminds us to "Wait for the LORD, and keep to His way, and He will exalt you" (Psalm 37:34), and St. Paul teaches us that love itself "is patient" (1 Corinthians 13:4).

Accountability

After you have prayerfully discerned what areas or topics are "non negotiables" for you in choosing a spouse, and if you still find yourself struggling with sticking to your standards, ask a close friend to be an accountability partner for you, and hold you to your standards at the beginning of each new relationship interest. Your accountability friend will help safeguard your heart from settling.

Remember That God Is In Control

The Author of Life is writing your life story, including the chapters of your love story. The hardest thing for a single person – or any Christian for that matter – is to surrender our will, our hopes, our dreams, and our desires to God, and let Him take control of our lives. This is really hard, but it's also really worth it.

"For I know the plans I have for you, says the LORD, plans for welfare and not for evil, to give you a future and a hope." – Jeremiah 29:11

Action Step

God's dreams for your life are even bigger than the ones you dream for yourself. Take courage, raise the bar high, and don't settle for anything less than His best for you. Reflect on which category you fall under: Picky, Too Picky, Not Picky Enough. Depending on which category you find yourself in, are there ways that you can adjust your outlook? Write down your priorities and ask a friend to give their advice on the reasonableness of your desires. Is your bar aimed too high or too low? A trusted friend or family member can help! Just ask.

PART FIVE

Praying For
The Right One

Chapter 23

Praying For Your Future Spouse

"Prayer is the place of refuge for every worry, a foundation for cheerfulness, a source of constant happiness, a protection against sadness."

— **Saint John Chrysostom**

"When I was younger and single, I used to go to daily Mass. I loved this gift of the single life and being able to receive the Eucharist every day. Many of my friends, single and married, were doing the same. One day, one of my friends who was married asked if I was involved with anyone on a serious level and I wistfully shook my head no.

"Don't worry," she told me. "It will happen but one of you isn't ready, yet. You should be praying for him because he's probably praying for you."

— **Lisa Duffy**

There are so many things in life you cannot control and the timing of meeting your spouse-to-be is certainly one of those things. For single people, this is the chief complaint; When will the love of my life show up? Wanting, waiting, hoping, searching is your daily bane. It's always a good thing to keep working toward your goals, but it's all in God's perfect timing, so in the meantime, you can work on the one thing in life you can control, yourself.

If you are prepared to meet your future spouse and you have all your ducks in a row, why not incorporate some daily prayer time for your future spouse?

No matter what type of prayer you offer for your future wife or future husband, make sure that in addition to praying for the right time to meet her or him, that you also pray for their growth in virtue and love for God; for their integrity, honesty, and leadership.

It's so important to have God be a part of every aspect of your relationship; dating, engagement and marriage. By praying for your future spouse, you now have a way to include God even in your preparation to meet.

Action Step

Praying for your future spouse is extremely powerful, making a spiritual bond before you have even met. One great way to do this is by praying a novena. There is one novena in particular that you can pray with many faithful Catholics around the world. It is a novena to the Blessed Mother called the Novena for Marriage and Family.

Chapter 24

Praying
To Find Love

"Pray with great confidence, with confidence based upon the goodness and infinite generosity of God and upon the promises of Jesus Christ. God is a spring of living water which flows unceasingly into the hearts of those who pray."

— *Saint Louis de Montfort*

Pope Francis tweeted a message on Twitter that is a great slogan for all single Catholics:

Christians are always full of hope; they should never get discouraged (@pontifex).

To be always full of hope and never discouraged—even when you're lonely and wondering when it will be your turn to find love—is a great witness to the world but admittedly one that isn't always easy to keep up. But it's a guidepost for those days when you just don't feel like putting a smile on your face.

Part 5 • Chapter 24

Prayer is the key to linking your yearning heart to the will of God and being able to tap into that hope that keeps you motivated and moving forward. Here is one woman's personal account of how prayer, particularly a novena to St. Anne, led her directly to her future husband. Here's how it happened for Annie Piekarczyk (now Deddens) in her own words:

I'm not always very patient, but I am diligent. About three years ago, I started praying to Saint Anne. I never knew too much about her, but a few girls I used to live with joked about asking Saint Anne to, "send me a man as fast as you can!" It was quick, catchy and it caught on.

At the time, I knew of another girl who also prayed to her and, who shortly thereafter, met her future boyfriend (and now husband). So I thought I would try it and see how things worked out—and let me tell you, it definitely worked out!

I prayed the novena to St. Anne a couple of times—and all the while, I had been growing in patience and learned to trust more in God's timing and His will for my life—not just for my heart.

I knew that I wanted to grow a relationship and build a career centered around my faith—rather than a faith that somehow worked itself around a relationship and a career. And I wanted to marry someone who shared those same values and the same faith—so that's what I was praying for.

It was maybe about a week after I finished the novena that I met John-Paul. I was working as a reporter at the time, and I actually ended up contacting him as a source for a pro-life campaign I was covering. We met for the interview—probably one of the longest interviews I've ever done (he's not a big talker—but he was talking a lot!). Afterwards, I turned off my recorder, was ready to go—but he surprised me and said, "So, tell me about yourself." The tables had been turned! I had been a reporter for a while—always the one asking questions, so this definitely made him stand out to me.

A couple months later, we began dating—we dated for about a year and a half before we got engaged. During that time, I continued to pray through St. Anne's intercession—her novena, among others, and those prayers *changed my life. I'm not sure I would have met John-Paul if I hadn't prayed to St. Anne and if I hadn't covered that pro-life campaign three years ago.*

What a beautiful story of romantic love that began with love for the will of God and acceptance of His timing. Not only did the habit of prayer lead them to find each other, but it also became the signature of their life as a couple.

Action Step

The website PrayMoreNovenas.Com is a site that Annie started with her husband. It is dedicated to helping people enrich their lives and discover God's will through prayer, specifically through novenas. The Novena to St. Anne is traditionally started on July 17th but you can say it at any time.

Chapter 25

Persevering
In Prayer

"Whether, therefore, we receive what we ask for, or do not receive it, let us still continue steadfast in prayer. For to fail in obtaining the desires of our heart, when God so wills it, is not worse than to receive it; for we know not as He does, what is profitable to us."

— *Saint John Chrysostom*

So what if you want to pray for God's will, but your prayers are always distracted? As it is with many things we want to improve, sometimes it's easier said than done and quite often when we take time to pray with the best of intentions, our thoughts run away from us. We can become totally focused on everything except prayer without even realizing it's happening.

For example, if you pray the Sorrowful mysteries of the Rosary and contemplate all that Christ suffered, you might envision a scene from the movie *The Passion of the Christ* because it is such a vivid and powerful depiction of Christ's passion. But then you might start imagining what it was like behind the scenes on that movie and what it might have been like to be on the set with Mel Gibson and Jim Caviezel. Then you might remember sitting in the theater watching that movie with a dear friend you haven't seen in a while and wonder how she's doing these days. You tell yourself how terrible you are for not sending her a Christmas card last year... By then you get to the last bead of that decade and wake up to the fact that you haven't focused on any of it! Does any of this sound familiar? If you struggle with being distracted in prayer, you are definitely not the only one.

But try not to beat yourself up about it. Persevere and refocus your sincere attention on the next mystery. It's important to remember that God does not expect us to be perfect in prayer, but He does want us to give our best effort.

It's like a bridegroom who wakes up on the day of his wedding and realizes he's overslept. He's late! What is his bride thinking? He races around getting his things in order and rushes to shower and dress. A few minutes later he runs out the door and gets into the car. As he drives away, he realizes he's forgotten his cuff links, but he can't stop and turn around. Better late with no cuff links than miss his own wedding. Suddenly, there is a loud noise and the car begins to bump violently. Flat tire! The bridegroom gets out of the car and getting out his tools and spare, changes the tire. Now, he is *really* late! But he presses on even though he knows his bride must be worried. Fifteen minutes later, he has tightened the last lug nut and put away his tools. Closing the trunk, he turns to get back in the car and as he approaches the driver's side door, a bus drives by, splattering him with mud. The bridegroom looks at his clothes, utterly distressed, but then hops in the car and races off.

Finally, he arrives at the church only to find the parking lot empty. Everyone has gone home. He hangs his head as he walks inside the church. He is sorrowful and afraid of what his bride might be thinking. As he walks up the aisle, the bride sees him from the altar where she has been sitting on the steps. She certainly felt he had changed his mind but when she sees him and his dirty clothes, his wrecked hair and the sadness on his face, she is filled with love for him. She doesn't care about the way he looks. He didn't stand her up! He still loves her! She can see what he's been through. The fact that he persevered and never gave up the fight to reach her, made her love him all the more.

This is a simple illustration but all the same, it is the way God sees us as we struggle with distractions in prayer. Our thoughts wander, we're distracted, we're late, stuff happens. But our imperfections are not what God takes note of. He is pleased by the fact that we don't give up. That's all he asks of us, that we persevere.

Action Step

Here are a few suggestions to help you remain focused in prayer:

- Ask God for the grace to stay focused.
- Pray in a place that is as distraction-free as possible.
- Don't get discouraged. If you find your thoughts wandering don't give up praying, just try again.

PART SIX

Looking At
The Bigger Picture

Chapter 26

How To Keep From Worrying About Tomorrow

"Pray, Hope, and Don't Worry."

— **Saint Pio of Pietrelcino**

"So are you seeing anyone?"

My face burns red hot and I feel the sweat running down my back. I can't even escape this question at the dentist office.

"No." I laugh nervously. "Do you know anyone?"

Then I wait for the I-feel-bad-for-you look to end so I can gracefully change the subject or run out of there as fast as I can.

I cringe every time the dating question comes up. What is the big deal? Why do I let it bother me so much?

Well, because I'm a worrier.

Even though I'm 20 minutes early, I worry I won't catch my train. Even though my nephew plays Irish football all the time, I worry that he will break his wrist. Even though I am only in my early 30s, I'm afraid that I will be single forever!

Maybe this sounds dramatic, but I do worry. **Why haven't I met someone? Did I miss God's plan for me?**

I carry all this worry into the adoration chapel and kneel in front of the blessed sacrament shouting my questions and demanding answers. But I hear nothing.

I then decide to flip to the readings for the next day. The Gospel was from Matthew (6:24-34):

"Therefore I tell you, do not worry about your life, ... Look at the birds in the sky; they do not sow or reap, they gather nothing into barns, yet your heavenly Father feeds them. Are you more important than they? Can any of you by worrying add a single moment to your life-span? ... But seek first the Kingdom of God and His righteousness, and all these things will be given you besides. Do not worry about tomorrow; tomorrow will take care of itself. Sufficient for a day is its own evil."

And then I knew I was exactly where I needed to be: At our Lord's feet, receiving His sweet consolation.

I was so focused on the day-to-day stresses that I forgot to put God first. His gentle reminder brought me a rush of peace. He was smiling down on me saying, "Don't worry. I know where we are going. Just follow me."

I don't know what bumps are on the road ahead. I don't know if I will be single tomorrow or for many tomorrows, but next time I hear the question, "Are you seeing anyone?" I'll know to say "I'm leaving it in God's hands and not worrying about tomorrow."

— ***Robyn Lee***

Action Step

Listening to music is a great way to find inspiration or take a break from worry:

- Rise Up by Matt Maher
- Your Grace is Enough by Matt Maher
- Lord, I Need You by Matt Maher
- Even in This by Josh Blakesley Band
- You're Not Alone by Marie Miller
- You Make the Most of Me by Marie Miller
- Love is Moving by Audrey Assad
- I Shall Not Want by Audrey Assad

Chapter 27

Living
A Life Of Love

"The perfection of life is the perfection of love. Love is the life of the soul."

— Saint Francis de Sales

"It was several years ago, during a time when I was really struggling with my "singleness." I was pouring my heart out to my spiritual director about how I hated the prospect of never marrying, how I was sick to death of only finding the "wrong" guys and even sicker to death of showing up at events alone, how every vision I had ever envisioned for my future revolved around children, and how a life without marriage felt to me like a life without love.

He listened sympathetically, and then we began to pray about it. I don't remember exactly how the praying went. But I do remember that, at the end, we both had a very clear sense that God had spoken. His response was this:

"Simple love is sufficient."

*"Simple love? What the heck is that? I want **love** love. You know, romance and fireworks and 'forsaking all others' and the whole package."*

"Simple love is sufficient."

So I was left with no choice but to confront the concept of "simple love." I had spent my entire adult life traveling around the world speaking to audiences about love. I knew what it was. And I knew there were different types of love—agape love, family love, friendship love, romantic love. Of all of them, "romantic" love—the love of a husband and a wife—was certainly the least simple. It involves the blending of two lives and the meshing of two egos. It's day-in-and-day-out "working it out," building a life together. It can be incredibly rewarding (or so I've heard), but it isn't simple.

I didn't have romantic love in my life, but I did—and do—have simple love. I have single and divorced friends who share my dateless Saturday nights and my lonely single moments. I have married friends who include me in their family dinners and their kids' birthday parties. I have brothers who have my back, and a sister who has made me an extended part of her family. I have nieces and nephews who call me "Bopper" (or "Mom . . . I mean Bop"), who I love like they were my own. And I have a 91 year old dad who still walks over to my house to put my cans away on trash day, and an 82 year old mother who still makes dinner for me when she's afraid I'm not eating well enough.

My life may be lacking in romantic love, but it is certainly not lacking in love.

It's not automatic. Like married love, "simple" love needs to be constantly cultivated. I need to **love**. I can't take friends or extended family for granted any more than I could take a spouse for granted. First, I need to force myself out of the cozy cocoon of my house, to meet people who may later come to join my circle of "simple *love." And once they are there, I need to love them, to think about how I can be God's love in their lives. I'm not saying I'm great at **any** of that, but I have realized I need to try.*

I know what you're saying: "But it's not the same!" Of course it's not the same. Having a lot of people in your life who care about you isn't the same as having one person who has given himself to you. Loving somebody else's kids isn't the same as loving your own kids. I get that. I feel that. I live that.

*But God didn't tell me it was the same. He didn't tell me it was ideal. He told me it was **sufficient.** He told me it was enough—that, if I would stop grasping for the one kind of love I didn't have and instead look around at all of the love I **did** have, I would find that there is great joy and happiness to be found in that "simple love."*

Of course I still have difficult moments, and lonely moments, and moments when I see clearly that this arrangement may be sufficient, but it is hardly ideal. But that—the gap between "sufficient" and "ideal"—is something I can offer to Him. It is in those moments, turning to Him in prayer, that I see most clearly that nothing in this life is "ideal," and that His is the only love that will ever fully satisfy.

I am not closed to the possibility that I may someday marry. Who knows what God has in store? But I do know that He gave me a great gift that day, when He shot down my silly notion that an unmarried life must be a "loveless" life, and opened my eyes to the love already surrounding me. He assured me that, when it comes to love, He will provide me—and you—with our "daily bread."

And He showed me that, for now, simple love is indeed sufficient."

— **Mary Beth Bonacci**

Action Step

Practice acts of simple love today. Send flowers to your mom. A card to your sister. Bring your dad to a baseball game. Shower your nieces and nephews with love and attention. Pick one day each week to devote to these special acts of love.

Chapter 28

Why Marriage Won't Solve Your Problems

"The more a person loves God, the more reason he has to hope in Him. This hope produces in the Saints an unutterable peace, which they preserve even in adversity, because as they love God, and know how beautiful He is to those who love Him, they place all their confidence and find all their repose in Him alone."

— *Saint Alphonsus Liguori*

Some people believe that marriage will solve their loneliness issues or will bring meaning to their seemingly boring lives.

However, only God can truly make us happy, fill our hearts, and make our lives complete! It would be a mistake to replace God with a human being. This expectation will always fail and end in disillusionment. We need to walk and grow side by side with our life partner and not be desperately dependent on them or overly needy.

"Only God can truly make us happy, fill our hearts, and make our lives complete!"

There is a difference between learning from each other's strengths and growing together, and then becoming dependent on another person—or visa versa. We need to become our own full person, a person fully alive, the whole person God has called us to be! So that even if we remained single for our whole life, we would still be working to better ourselves daily.

It is important to find healthy individuals who are their own person first, and who can stand on their own two feet. They are already working on their own problems, vices, and shortcomings, and are making progress.

For example, if they aren't good at communication or showing affection, they don't make excuses for it, they work toward fixing the problem. The same goes for us too.

After all, marriage is a lifelong endeavor of helping each other get to heaven and become better people. Therefore, it is so important to find someone who shares the same morals, values, standards, and desires for your faith that you do.

Not only do they share them, but they are actively working toward them in their own lives. Two healthy people who share a common vision and who grow and learn together will help to make a lasting marriage. It will also make the journey to heaven more beautiful and enjoyable.

Action Step

Take a moment to reflect - are you dependent on other people in an unhealthy way? If the answer is yes, write down the ways that you are too dependent. Now write down the ways you can work towards independence in these areas. Do you rely on a certain person to make you happy? The next time you are sad, try to lighten your mood completely on your own - through prayer, exercise, music, or a drive around the block. Practice this type of healthy independence in each area of your life. Kindly explain to the people close to you what you are trying to achieve and why. Hopefully if they are true friends, they will help you work towards achieving a healthy balance in your life.

Chapter 29

Embracing
The Life You Are Meant To Lead

"Be who God meant you to be and you will set the world on fire."

— *Saint Catherine of Siena*

I've been asked many times in the past the burning question of 'Is Single Life a Vocation?' (Short answer, "no.") It crops up repeatedly, and to be quite honest I've never really understood why some people get so emotional about it.

Until now.

I was talking to a friend, who told me that she recently attended a Catholic conference. And, at that conference, one of the sessions was led by a very young, starry-eyed little engaged couple who spoke about the urgency with which they pursued marriage because they didn't want to somehow "miss" their vocations and hence "waste their lives."

Seriously?

Look, I wasn't there, so everything I'm hearing is second-hand. But if these two people indeed said anything close to what I'm hearing they said, their Catholic Speaker Union Membership Cards should be permanently revoked. And perhaps burned.

Is this why single Catholics get so revved up about the question of whether unconsecrated single life is a vocation? Have others of you been hearing that your vocation-less lives are wasted?

We need to clear this up once and for all.

*The Church says that we were created to find fulfillment through giving ourselves in love, to "find ourselves through a sincere gift of ourselves" as **Gaudium et Spes** so beautifully puts it. And the Church teaches that there are two "vocations," two ways to **give** the entirety of our lives. We can either give ourselves to a spouse in marriage, or to God in the religious life. Each of us is "called" to one of these two vocations, these two ways of permanently, irrevocably giving ourselves.*

And, in a perfect world, each of us would understand exactly which vocation we have been called to, and would have all of the means at our disposal to respond to that call.

Unfortunately, we do not live in a perfect—or even a near-perfect—world. We live in a world hampered by original sin. And hence, entering into those vocations can be easier said than done. Sometimes it's our own brokenness that gets in the way. (Fear of commitment, sexual problems, circumstantial issues, etc.) Other times it's the brokenness in others and in the world. (Decline in religious practice, difficulty in meeting others who share faith, spousal abuse or abandonment leading to separation, etc.) Most often it's probably a little (or a lot) of both.

*But here's the point. (And I'm writing it in all caps because, yes, I'm yelling.) A LIFE LIVED OUTSIDE OF A VOCATION IS NOT A LIFE WASTED. Such a life, of course, **can** be wasted—as can a life lived within a marriage or the religious life. It's not whether* *we're married or single or religious that determines whether we're "wasting" our lives. It's more about **how** we live in whatever state we find ourselves. Do we love? Do we seek to give ourselves, or merely to pursue our own satisfaction? Do we seek God's guidance? Do we listen to His voice?*

*If someone said "I have no interest in getting married because I'm inherently selfish and I'd rather just focus on myself," I would say that person was on the way to a wasted life. But I'd say that same to the princess who marries the rich guy just for the perks, or the guy who treats his wife as a short order cook or a breeding machine. A selfish life is a wasted life. But, the thing is, the singles I know **aren't** single because they're selfish. The selfish ones exist, I'm sure, but I don't know them. The singles I know would like to be married, would love to give themselves and their lives to someone who would treasure the gift and reciprocate the love.*

"A life lived outside of a vocation is not a life wasted."

But, in this day and age, that can be easier said than done.

*As I've pointed out before, St. Paul tells us that "ALL things work together for good for those who love Him, who walk according to His ways." (Rom 8:28) He knew from all eternity what would happen in your life. And He's here now to meet you in the midst of it, and to make it into something beautiful for Him. All that is necessary for that to happen is for us to pursue what the Church has always said is our **primary** vocation, the vocation to holiness. We are called to pursue Him, to allow Him to transform us more fully into His image, and to "walk according to His ways."*

*If you are doing that, I can absolutely assure you that you are **not** "wasting your life."*

— **Mary Beth Bonacci**

Action Step

By seeking God's will and walking in Christ's footsteps, you are following the path God has set out for you. Renew your commitment to live a full life of love, hope, and service. How is God calling you? Write down ideas of things that you can do to build up the Kingdom of God. First work on your own relationship with Christ. Then look outward and see the needs of your church and community. Service is needed in so many ways! Missionaries, CCD teachers, pantry volunteers, prison ministry. There are countless ways to share your love of Christ and minister to the less fortunate. Pick one thing that you are interested in doing. If it is teaching CCD, contact the parish DRE and find out if they need help. I guarantee they'll be looking for teachers! Whatever it is, follow through with your plan. Check back in one month.

Conclusion

You are on a journey. The journey to find love. This journey began a long time ago when the Author of Love breathed life into you. And with that life, He gave you a special mission. A mission to love.

That mission is found in your heart - God, Himself, placed it there. You were made to know and love God. There lies your happiness. But God did not make us to travel this journey alone. He made us to live in friendship with each other. He also designed a special lifelong covenant between a man and a woman that would mirror His own life-giving love.

You may have just set off on your journey, or you may be a well-seasoned traveler. Along the way, surely there have been bumps and bruises. Some you have certainly weathered unscathed, but others have made their marks. Those marks have taught you many lessons. Some are good lessons, but as you travel on, they affect how you live your life. Though you carry on, it is with more caution, reserve, and fear.

And this is where trust comes in. You trust that a great and loving Father is ever-present, guiding you on the road. And while that road seems long, and sometimes winding, you know that your path was carefully chosen just for you by the One who created you. And for some, the path is short, while for others it is quite long. Some will lose their way, while others will remain steadfast, though the path is steep. And some will have a helper along the way. Every path is unique, but one thing is the same—it is this path, that if we choose to follow well, will lead us to our goal: ultimate union with God.

We hope *The Catholic's Guide to Being Single* will be valuable to you as you discover God's plan. Go back and read it again and again for inspiration, and ideas. Take the time to go back through the chapters and perform the action steps. These will help you grow in your faith, and as a person. They will also help you meet other single Catholics that are on the journey as well. And God willing, someone who will share your path to eternity.

The CatholicMatch Institute would like to thank the contributors of *The Catholic's Guide to Being Single*. This guide would not be complete without their wisdom and support.

Robyn Lee, Lisa Duffy, Mary Beth Bonacci, Bryan Mercier, Jessica Weinberger, Amy Smith, Anastasia Northrop, Danielle Bean, Susie Lloyd, Stephanie Wood Weinert, Brian Barcaro.

Visit the CatholicMatch Institute blog where we offer advice on dating, spirituality, single living and more (www.CatholicMatchInstitute.com).

PART ACKNOWLEDGEMENTS

Thanks Folks!

Deanna and Michael experienced a mutual dream come true when they had the opportunity to meet Pope Francis!

A Story of Love, Hope and Meeting the Pope!

By Lori Hadacek Chaplin,
CatholicMatch Institute

Deanna, 24, and Michael, 24, had never dated before they met each other on CatholicMatch. Michael had been discerning the priesthood for four years, and it seems God had placed a bubble around lovely Deanna—saving her just for Michael.

They were married on October 5, 2013, in her home parish in Memphis, TN. CatholicMatch talked with Deanna about her initial reservations about joining an online dating site, about her online dating experience, having her marriage blessed by Pope Francis, and more.

Why did you join CatholicMatch?

In 2010, I was 24 and had never dated. This was not by my own choice, and it was frustrating. Where were the good Catholic men? Was there something wrong with me? What I didn't realize at the time was that God was writing a better story than I ever could have imagined.

Online dating was something I said I would never do. I think I had my hopes set on running into "The One" at Mass, or maybe at my local Starbucks! My perception of online dating changed in part because a friend that I really admired met her spouse on a Catholic dating site. So maybe it wasn't that bad after all, but I still held out hope that I would meet my husband in a more "traditional" way.

My decision to join CatholicMatch was a slow one, but I think the ball really got rolling when I attended the 2010 National Catholic Singles Conference in San Antonio. Brian Barcaro gave a talk about online dating and why he started CatholicMatch. Alright, I thought, maybe this wasn't such a crazy idea, but I still needed more time.

A few weeks after the Singles Conference, I finally hit my frustration point. "OK, God, if you're not going to send me anyone, I'm going to take matters into my own hands!" (As if I was the one arranging all of this...) At the beginning of March, I created my account and paid for a two-month membership.

How long were you a member before you met Michael?

I had been a member for about five or six weeks when I first saw Michael's picture. Around the middle of April, I saw the "New Members" feature and there was a picture of a guy with a nice smile holding what looked like a baby leopard (extra points for a unique profile picture!). After glancing through Michael's profile, I decided I would send him a message with a nice smiley face at the end, but I didn't really expect a reply.

Never underestimate the power of a smile!

This would be the first of many messages we would exchange over the next few weeks. By the end of April, we were emailing one another once or twice a day with questions and answers on everything under the sun. By July 2, we officially started dating.

There's no doubt in my mind that God's hand was part of all of this. His timing is perfect, and Michael was definitely worth the wait!

> *I think it's really interesting to see how God's hand has been part of our entire relationship, and how everything happened in His perfect timing.*

What drew you to Michael?

I think the first thing that caught my attention about Michael, even before we started emailing each other, was his sense of humor. His profile expressed his deep love for chocolate milk and Haribo gummy bears, and the quiz he wrote showed his creative and quirky imagination.

I could also tell that this man really loved Jesus and his Catholic faith. He had spent four years in seminary before discerning that the priesthood was not his vocation, and he was ready to discern the vocation to marriage. I appreciated the fact that he had never been in a relationship either, and that we were essentially stepping into the unknown world of dating and relationships together.

He wasn't just looking for a fling; we were really discerning marriage. Michael has always kept Christ at the center of our relationship, and that definitely made him a keeper!

Any interesting or funny stories about your online dating experience?

One of the memories that still makes me smile are those initial emails we exchanged. After sending a few back and forth, Michael thought he would answer my questions in an audio recording, and I recorded my answers. So we sent MP3s back and forth a few times before Michael finally just asked for my phone number.

Our first two-and-a-half years of dating were pretty much long distance, but I think this actually made our relationship stronger because we talked so often. Communication became a key part of our relationship. That's a benefit of online dating really, especially at the beginning of the relationship. You're forced to talk to each other and the physical doesn't get in the way of getting to know the other person.

I think it's really interesting to see how God's hand has been part of our entire relationship, and how everything happened in His perfect timing. A year after we started dating, we enrolled in a graduate theology program through Newman University in Wichita, which meant we got to see one another every few months or so for class.

God really did make a way for us to continue this courtship despite the distance.

How did Michael propose?

Right after the Easter Vigil Mass on March 30, 2013, Michael and I were taking pictures with a friend of ours who had just joined the Church.

We posed for the picture, but right before the photo was taken Michael said, "Deanna?" I turned towards him and said, "Yes?" right as he was getting down on one knee. I was shocked and teary-eyed, but once Michael asked the question, I said, "Yes!" That's when I realized that the people standing around the altar were taking pictures and video taping of the proposal.

One of the things I love about the pictures from our engagement is that Michael proposed at the foot of the altar, and in the picture you can see the tabernacle right in between us. Our prayer is that the Eucharist always remains at the center of our family.

When in Rome, do as the Romans do! Deanna and Michael sightseeing on their honeymoon in Italy

What was it like having your marriage blessed by Pope Francis?

On October 16, Michael and I attended the papal audience in St. Peter's Square. We were able to obtain Sposi Novelli (Newlywed) tickets, which meant that we were invited to wear our wedding attire to the audience and sit in a special section that was a little bit closer to the Holy Father.

After the Pope's address, the Vatican security guards instructed us to file out of the section. I assumed that meant everything was over now and it was time to go home. Then we realized they were taking us to Pope Francis! Before we knew it, we were standing at the center of the platform waiting for the Holy Father to come and greet us.

As Pope Francis shook Michael's hand, I said in Spanish, "Holy Father, we are from the United States. We are praying for you." Pope Francis shook my hand, and then Michael handed him a holy card that we had given to our wedding guests, which has a picture of the Divine Mercy. I told the Holy Father, "This is a gift from our wedding. We were married on October 5, the feast of St. Faustina." Pope Francis looked at both sides of the card, smiled, and then he made his way to the next couple in line. Michael and I stood there for a moment, a bit awestruck at what had just happened.

When I think about our wedding reception and the brief moments I was able to spend personally greeting our guests, I think about our moment with Pope Francis. The Pope had to have greeted hundreds of people before he came to us. He wasn't just shaking hands and kissing babies because of some kind of obligatory papal duty. Rather, he greeted each person, and he looked at each one of us like a father lovingly looks at his children. Even though he didn't say a word, he listened to us. He looked at us. He smiled at us. In that moment, he was present to each person, sharing the love and joy of Christ, even if it was only with a smile.

Looking back at the pictures that were taken of us with Pope Francis, I still find it hard to believe that we were able to experience something so special. The Holy Father gave us just a few seconds of his time, but he taught us that sharing the joy of our faith can be as simple as being joyful and fully present to each person we encounter. This is one of the best wedding presents we could have ever received.

catholicmatch
INSTITUTE

Our mission: Preparing singles, supporting couples, and helping Church leaders foster healthy marriages. To promote CatholicMatch Institute in your parish or diocese visit: www.CatholicMatchInstitute.com or call: 888.267.8885 x3

Parish Resources For
Dating & Marriage

Top 10 Reasons You Should Get Married

Danielle Bean, Catholic Digest publisher and mother of eight, gives the top 10 reasons that every person not called to religious life should consider marriage a worthy goal.

7 Tips for Newly Married Couples

This guide is specifically geared toward couples in the first years of marriage. It asks some tough questions that will require honest answers of the couple.

Purposeful Dating for Catholics

This practical resource helps single Catholics better discern dating and marriage as well as grow deeper in their faith.

To order copies individually or in bulk
visit CatholicMatchInstitute.com or call 888•267•8885 x 3

PART MORE

Thanks for reading
The Catholic's Guide To Being Single.

For more resources on dating and marriage, visit our website:
www.CatholicMatchInstitute.com

Made in the USA
Lexington, KY
30 September 2018